D1764960

Encounters of a Mathematician

Walter Ledermann

Published in 2009 by Walter Ledermann,
25 Highpoint, North Hill,
London, N6 4BA, England
Telephone (+44) 20 8347 9062

Copyright © 2009 Walter Ledermann

All Rights Reserved.

No part of this publication may be reproduced, stored in a retrieval system or transmitted
in any form or by any means, electronic, mechanical, photocopying, recording, scanning or
otherwise, except under the terms of the Copyright, Designs and Patents Act 1988 or
under the terms of a license issued by the Copyright Licensing Agency, without the
permission in writing of the Publisher.

This publication is designed to provide accurate and authoritative information in regard to
the subject matter covered. It is sold on the understanding that the Publisher is not
engaged in rendering professional services. If professional advice or other expert assistance
is required, the services of a competent professional should be sought.

Walter Ledermann has asserted his right under the Copyright, Designs and Patents Act
1988, to be identified as the author of this work.

ISBN 978-1-4092-8267-9

Printed and bound in the United States of America by Lulu..

Encounters of a Mathematician

Contents

Childhood in Berlin	1
Mathematical Awakening and Musical Abundance	7
The Formative Years: Berlin, 1928 – 33	23
Emigration: St. Andrews, 1934 – 36	44
Edinburgh, 1936 – 8 and Thereafter	58
Start of my Academic Career	72
War Experiences and Marriage	82
Manchester, 1946 – 62	91
Sussex, 1962 – 97	109
Final Retirement: London 1997	130

Acknowledgments

I am profoundly grateful to Professor Geoffrey Howson, Dr Steven Nicholls and Professor Edmond Robertson for helping me to make much needed improvements of an earlier version of these memoirs. Their painstaking work was invaluable to me. I am also deeply indebted to Professor Carol Alexander for preparing the e-version and making the book available on the internet. Above all, I express my heartfelt thanks to my son, Jonathan whose advice and work contributed significantly to the final version.

Preface

"Mathematics is a soulless occupation devoid of feeling and human values". This or similar opinions are often expressed. Mathematics is certainly disliked by many. Morris Kline quotes St. Augustine as stating: "the good Christian should beware of mathematicians. ... The danger already exists that the mathematicians have made a covenant with the devil to darken the spirit and to confine man in the bonds of hell". [1]

Perhaps mathematicians are unpopular because they use a language that is inaccessible to others, or at least had caused them much pain at school. On the other hand, it is this secret language that fosters in the mathematical community a feeling of solidarity and comradeship.

Moreover, there are no controversies or polemics in mathematics – excepting a few cases in the past when some branches of mathematics impinged on philosophy and a few mathematicians were not on speaking terms because they had different notions of infinity.

Now we may safely assume that when two mathematicians talk about their work they will listen to each other without prejudice and are glad to share ideas. Most of my contributions to research were the result of interaction with scholars of an older generation or with friends and colleagues.

The task of communicating mathematics has occupied me throughout my professional life. I enjoy lecturing to students and I am pleased to meet them individually. At a different level I am keen to explain mathematical concepts and results to people who are not mathematicians, but who have to use mathematics in their professional work.

In contrast to the opinions quoted at the beginning of this Preface, I feel strongly that mathematics can and should form part of human relationships. The encounters I have had in my career

---

[1] Morris Kline, *Mathematics in Western Culture* (Penguin Books, 1972), page 19

iii

have been invaluable to me, and I am happy to recall them. The purpose of this book is to emphasize the human dimension of mathematics, and I dedicate it in gratitude to my teachers, colleagues and students.

Walter Ledermann, May 2009

I
Childhood in Berlin

I was born in 1911, as the second of the four children of William and Charlotte Ledermann. My father was a physician who had a busy medical practice in a humble working class district of Berlin. It was part of his duties to care for the poorest members of the community. All his patients were very devoted to him. As a young bachelor doctor in the 1890s he started his medical practice in a small apartment on the first floor of a block of flats each consisting of a room and a kitchen. This was all that a working class family could afford at that time.

William Ledermann 1871-1949   Charlotte Ledermann neé Apt 1883-1979

There was no sanitation in the flats, the communal lavatories being situated on the main stairway half-a-level below the living quarters. When my father got married to Charlotte Apt and in due course the children were born, he repeatedly acquired more units of kitchen-plus-living-room, until we occupied the whole of the first floor of the block, about ten rooms in all. Some of the kitchens were turned into bathrooms which were utterly unknown elsewhere in the block. Three rooms were used for the medical practice, comprising a waiting room, an office and a treatment room. These were separated by a double door from the rest of the flat, which comprised our private rooms.

I was born in this apartment, as were my brother and sisters (hospital confinements were much less frequent in those days) and I lived there, until almost twenty-three years later, when I emigrated to Scotland. Thus all my childhood memories and my development into adulthood are associated with this place.

The apartment was situated in a corner house. There were entrances either from 75, Wrangelstrasse, or from 17, Cuvrystrasse; we had in fact three main entrance doors at the street level. Our apartment was reached in one flight of stairs, passing the communal lavatory half way. All the rooms were on the same level above the street. They were joined by a long corridor which consisted of two parts at a right angle to each other, following the shape of the corner house. We were not unduly troubled by the fact that the apartment was situated in a rather miserable part of Berlin and that an evil smell frequently issued from another part of the building. By way of compensation, there was a large public park in the vicinity where we regularly played with our childhood friends.

When our family was complete, seven persons lived in this apartment (I give the year of birth in brackets): my father William (1871), my mother Charlotte (1883), the four children: Erich (1908), Walter (1911), Käte (1914) and Ruth (1922). In addition, Aunt Recha (1863) lived with us. She was the eldest of my father's four sisters. Two of them had died as young women; a third sister, Eugenie, had married an American and lived in San Francisco. None of them had children. I never saw Aunt Eugenie but I have fond memories about her, because she very kindly sent us parcels from America after the First World War, when food was still scarce in Germany. It was the first time that I saw and tasted chocolate when these parcels arrived.

Aunt Recha played an important part in my life. She was a kind of grandmother to me, both my real grandmothers having died in the first year of my life. When I was very young, Aunt Recha took me to the Synagogue on Friday evenings. Little boys were allowed to sit with the women. I was fascinated by the music and thrilled that I was allowed to sip a little wine at the Kiddush. In 1938, when my parents finally decided to leave Germany and join Erich and me in Britain, it was not feasible to bring Aunt Recha with them. She was put in an old-age home from where the Nazis deported and killed her.

We had an active social life. My mother had two brothers, Richard and Ernst and a sister, Hanna. They all had children, so I had uncles, aunts and cousins, most of whom I saw from time to time. I was fond of Aunt Hanna. As a young woman she had married Karl Gärtner and they had a son, Hans (1908). Sadly Hanna's husband died suddenly in 1914 and she did not remarry for many years. Hans was my favourite cousin, almost like a second brother to me. When he settled in Israel, he changed his name to Yochanan Ginat. In addition to their relatives, my parents had also friends who formed part of our family circle. Thea Jacobius - Aunt Thea to us children - was a life-long friend of my mother. An unmarried lady of high intelligence and warm feeling, she taught modern languages at a prestigious girls school in Berlin. It was always a great pleasure when Aunt Thea visited our family. It was tragic that the attempt to obtain for her an entry visa to Britain, even as a 'domestic servant' was unsuccessful. The Nazis deported her to the East, where she was murdered.

My mother's elder brother, Richard Apt took a doctorate in Physics at the University of Berlin. He was offered a professorship at one of the smaller German universities but he declined it because he suffered from a minor speech defect and felt uncomfortable about giving lectures. Instead he became an industrial physicist, rising to a directorship of an important cable works that had been founded by Emil Rathenau, the father of Walther Rathenau who was assassinated in 1922. When the Nazis came to power Richard unwisely transferred his office to Holland. When the Nazis occupied Holland, they arrested him and incarcerated him in the Belsen Concentration Camp where he died shortly before the camp was liberated by the British army.

My paternal grandfather was Jakob Ledermann. He died before I was one year old. From all the accounts I have gathered he must have been a remarkable man. As a young man he was a teacher in a small town near Pozan, in an Eastern province of Germany which later became part of Poland. Many of the children spoke Polish, and my grandfather was bilingual. Indeed, I was told that he was fluent in six languages, and that he had taught himself to play the violin and was proficient in short-hand writing. Being dissatisfied with his profession he moved with his family to Berlin. There he was engaged as a secretary by the banker Baron Bleichröder, who was not only Bismarck's personal banker, but also his confidant and friend. It would seem that sometimes Bleichröder used my grandfather as a 'secret agent'. On one of these occasions he sent him to Venice in connection with an intrigue designed to prevent the marriage of Bismarck's son to a lady of whom Bismarck strongly disapproved.[2]

Around 1870 my grandfather went to Britain. I do not know what the purpose of his visit was; but he returned full of admiration of what he had seen and experienced. "This is the country in which I should like to live" he declared, "there is freedom and respect for everybody, including Jews". Shortly afterwards his only son, my father, was born. He gave him the English name William. His plan to move to England with his family was not carried out. But by a twist of fate, my parents did in fact come to England when fleeing from the Nazis. They joined my brother and me here. Thus my grandfather's wish has been fulfilled to the extent that all his male descendants live in England.

My mother's background was very different from that of my father. Her father was Sigismund Apt, a wealthy metal merchant. He lived in a fashionable part of Berlin and also owned a country house in Hanhnenklee which is in the Harz mountains in central Germany, where members of the family and their friends would gather during the summer holidays.

Although I was only four years old when the First World War started, a few vivid memories remain: the sadness when my father

---

[2] Fritz Stern, *Gold and Iron* (A.A.Knopf, New York ,1977) , page 257

was called up to serve as a medical officer in the German army; the jubilation when Russia was defeated and I was allowed to take part in a torch light procession; I remember the revolution following the defeat of Germany. For a time Berlin was ruled by revolutionary gangs. When my father returned to Berlin after demobilization, the officer's insignia were torn from his uniform (he had rank of a captain) but he was allowed to keep the ceremonial sword, because he had paid for it with his own money. I was told that we no longer had a Kaiser and I could not believe that life without a Kaiser would be possible.

We were always conscious of being Jewish; but we were truly assimilated into German culture. We regarded ourselves as Germans until the time when the Nazis seized power. Only pure German was spoken in our family; we were not acquainted with Yiddish. We belonged to the association, whose members described themselves as "German citizens of the Jewish faith". My father had a somewhat orthodox upbringing. Throughout his life he went to the Synagogue on the High Holidays when my brother or I would accompany him and he fasted on Yom Kippur. But we did not celebrate the Sabbath nor did we insist on kosher food. However, every year some distant relatives invited us to Seder on Passover.

Both my brother and I had bar mitzvah ceremonies. Curiously, in my case it was held one year later than usual, when I was fourteen years old. My performance at the synagogue was minimal: I only had to say a blessing in Hebrew and then took no further part in the proceedings. But my parents gave a party to celebrate my bar mitzvah and I received many presents from relatives and friends of the family.

My mother appeared to have no interest in the Jewish religion. At her father's request she was exempt from taking part in Jewish instruction at school because it was his opinion that "if my daughter wants to pray to God, then she can pray in German." Initially, my parents did not support Zionism. But when the threat from the Nazis became ever more real, my sister Käte joined a Zionist youth group, and Ruth followed her in due course. They both emigrated to Palestine/Israel as soon as it was possible and settled there. We are very pleased to keep in touch with our family in Israel.

I started school at the age of six, as was the custom in Germany. This was still during the First World War. I attended the Preliminary School of the Köllnische Gymnasium (how odd that the Germans use the word gymnasium for a Grammar School, whereas in fact it means a place where naked boys are engaged in physical exercise). Incidentally, in mediaeval times, Kölln was a town twinned with Berlin; it had nothing to do with Köln, or Cologne, the principal city in the Rhineland.

I do not remember much about my early school years except that our teacher was a kind old gentleman. I was often absent on account of illness, because I had contracted chronic asthma when I was two years old. When I was seven, I was taken out of school for a whole term and put into the care of a farmer and his wife in Upper Silesia, close to what was soon to become the Polish frontier. I settled down well in the rustic surroundings. My task was to look after the geese, and the church warden gave me some lessons in writing and reading. When, three months later, my mother came to take me home, she could hardly understand me because I had picked up the local accent so thoroughly.

II
Mathematical Awakening and Musical Abundance

Soon after the war the Köllnische Gymnasium was closed by the new Socialist government and turned into an educational establishment for the less privileged members of the community. I became a pupil at the Leibniz Gymnasium in Belleallllianz Platz. This, too, was a conventional grammar school, in which boys from the ages of nine to eighteen received a secondary education with strong emphasis on the classics. In a bizarre manner the nine classes were numbered in Latin from six to one, in the reverse order, the most junior form being the sixth form, and the three top forms being divided into lower and upper classes, each running for two years. So the names of the nine classes from the bottom upwards were: sexta, quinta, quarta, lower tertia, upper tertia, lower secunda, upper secunda, lower prima, upper prima. Latin was studied for nine years and Greek for six years, each with at least six lessons a week. It is therefore not surprising that little time was left for the more modern aspects of education. However, French was taught from the third year onwards, though mostly for the purpose of reading rather than speaking the language. Despite the strong political antagonism, the view was still widely held in Germany that France was the centre of European civilization and that every cultured person should have knowledge of French. Unbelievably, English was almost totally ignored. During the last three years pupils were offered either English or Hebrew, at two lessons per week. The Hebrew option was not intended for the Jewish pupils, of whom there were only a small number, but for those who wanted to become ministers in the Protestant Church; for they were required to know enough Hebrew and Greek to read the Old and the New Testament in their original languages.

In schools of this kind mathematics was usually regarded as a topic of secondary importance. However, the Leibniz Gymnasium was exceptional in this respect; it had taken its name from one of the greatest German mathematicians, and it was considered a matter of honour and pride that a high standard in mathematics should be attained. Geometry was introduced in the third year (the quarta).

When I reached this stage in 1922, there was still a shortage of teachers with academic qualifications because training had been disrupted by the Great War. So, my first mathematics lesson was given by the Arts teacher, a benevolent elderly gentleman called Herr **Wüster**. In his teaching he closely followed the prescribed textbook which, according to custom in those days, was a simplified version of Euclid. After producing the usual definitions of a straight line, parallels and angles, Mr. Wüster reached the first substantial theorem, namely, that in every triangle the sum of the angles equals two right-angles. Although this is not a world-shaking fact, it had the quality of universal and unassailable truth, which impressed me greatly. The statement refers to all triangles whether drawn in the past or in the future. I realized that mathematical results possess an absolute certainty, that make them superior to the dogmas of philosophy and religion, which we are expected to accept 'without proof'. It was there and then that I decided to become a mathematician and I am grateful to Herr Wüster for having kindled the flame of enthusiasm.

Later on, two academically trained mathematicians were added to the teaching staff of the Leibniz Gymnasium. One of them was Herr **Anders**. He had been a naval officer in the War and conducted his lessons with military precision and efficiency. He demanded strict discipline. When the bell rang at the end of the lesson he called out in a clipped voice "stand up – class dismissed". Anders was an ardent nationalist and later supported the Nazis. But he was not unfair to me and even, at my father's request, supplied a six-line testimonial stating that my performance in mathematics had been "very good". Shortly after my emigration to Britain a former classmate spoke to Anders and, incidentally, expressed regret that I had left the country, to which Anders replied curtly "when you plane down wood, there will be shavings".

The other mathematician was Herr **Satow**. He was a good mathematician of flamboyant temperament. He boasted that he had studied very advanced mathematics at the University, including elliptic functions – but he never explained to us what they were. I enjoyed Satow's lessons; they were both instructive and entertaining. His real passions were mountaineering and the operas of Richard Wagner and Richard Strauss (he never mentioned Mozart or Verdi). His lessons were interspersed with accounts of his latest exploits in the Austrian Alps, or with lengthy quotations from Wagner's *Ring des Nibelungen*. "Boys, what was the most important event of the year 1911?" Answer: "The first performance of *Der Rosenkavalier*." On the whole, I benefited from Satow's lessons and I am grateful that I received a good mathematical education at the Leibniz Gymnasium, true to the spirit of its patron.

Although mathematics was my main interest, I also derived some enjoyment from studying the classics, especially Greek, when the teacher guided us through some of the original works of Homer, Sophocles and Plato. At one stage we were told to select our own project, and I presented Euclid's proof of Pythagoras's theorem in the original language.

There were only a few Jewish pupils at the Leibniz Gymnasium, but there were some Jewish teachers at the school, two of whom had a strong influence on my education; Herr Moritz **Baum** taught me Latin for several years and at one time was our 'Form Master' (Klassen Lehrer); he was a very efficient teacher. Herr Bruno **Strauss**, who later emigrated to the United States, taught German literature and impressed me with his original approach and insight.

On the whole I received a good general education at the Leibniz Gymnasium. Since I received good reports both in the classics and in mathematics, I was allowed to skip six months in the top form. I was therefore awarded the *leaving certificate* at an earlier age than would normally be the case. Consequently, I was able to complete my university course just before the Nazis would have forced me to abandon my studies.

I encountered no anti-Semitic aggression at school. On the contrary, I was on good terms with all my classmates. They appointed me to be their representative ('Speaker') when they wanted to make some requests to the teacher. Some of the hefty

Nordic lads, quite voluntarily and without being asked by me, undertook to be my bodyguard. I remember one occasion, when a boy from another class tried to bully me in the playground. He was immediately set upon by my protectors and beaten up.

One of my fellow pupils at the Leibniz Gymnasium was Walter Jakob, a typical German boy. He wrote exquisite German in a delicate handwriting but spoke it with a careless Berlin accent, which amused my mother. Jakob's father was killed in France while serving in the German army during the First World War. Walter was an only child living with his mother in very modest circumstances. I believe she made ends meet by doing other people's washing. My parents liked Walter and my mother invited him to join us for lunch on any Sunday he would like to come. He accepted this invitation quite frequently. Our friendship continued after we had both left the Leibniz Gymnasium and were both students at the University of Berlin. Walter was a devout Christian and wanted to become a Minister at a Protestant church. For this reason he had chosen the Hebrew option at our school and had learned to read the Old Testament in Hebrew.

While Walter was immersed in theology and I in mathematics it seemed that we had little in common. So Walter suggested that we should read the bible together in the original languages. I confessed that my knowledge was insufficient for this purpose. At my bar mitzvah service I had only to say the blessing in Hebrew and I was exempt from reciting part of the Old Testament in Hebrew. But Walter was not deterred. He offered to teach me enough Hebrew so that we could read some of the Old Testament in the original language. To this day I have a German-Hebrew dictionary which was compiled by a Christian theologian. After some time Walter suggested that we should move on to the New Testament. I had no difficulty with the original Greek text, since we had learned classical Greek for six years at our school. Apart from my religious feeling, I enjoyed reading the bible and even now sometimes revert to it using the authorized English translation. After all, it is the most successful book ever written.

My school years 1920-1928 were a period of much political unrest and tribulation in Germany. Soon after the end of the war there were clashes between the army and revolutionary groups who tried to establish a soviet-style regime. The Leibniz Gymnasium was within walking distance from my home. I remember some days when, on my way to school, I heard shouts "clear the streets" and I ran for shelter in a nearby house, before the army sprayed the street with machine gun fire in order to drive back its opponents.

For some time I was haunted by the death of Rosa Luxenburg, the communist revolutionary. She was murdered by army officers and her body was thrown into the Landwehr canal that traverses Berlin. The swimming bath, to which my father took us every day in the summer, was situated on the same canal, and I was afraid that the body of the dead woman would come up just when I was doing my exercises in the water.

Atrocities committed by right-wing fanatics were not just directed against communists. In June 1922 Walther Rathenau, the German foreign minister, was assassinated. "This is the beginning of the end", my father remarked prophetically, when he heard the news. It was no coincidence that both Luxenburg and Rathenau were Jews. The people who committed these crimes would soon form the nucleus of the Nazi party. In fact, it was in the following year that Hitler was involved in the unsuccessful violent attempt to overthrow the Bavarian government. The political situation rapidly deteriorated. The French occupied the Ruhr district, where much of Germany's industry was situated. This drastic action was taken, ostensibly, because Germany had failed to fulfil its obligation for restitution. This greatly increased the anger and the hatred towards the French, caused by what the Germans regarded as deliberate humiliation. I remember one morning the words of our modern language teacher, who had lost his right arm in the war. He was asked by the headmaster to take our class into the school hall for an assembly and I heard him mutter: "I would much rather lead you into battle against the French". We were then 14 years old.

About that time, R. Weizenböck published his important treatise on *The Theory of Invariants*. If one underlines the first letter of each sentence in the Preface, one would compose the words "Nieder mit den Franzosen", ("Down with the French")!

Of all the political calamities that befell Germany in those years, it is the run-away inflation of 1922-3 that left me with the most vivid and poignant memories. The value of the currency declined so rapidly that the exchange rate of the American dollar was officially quoted twice a day and displayed in shop windows. Wages had to be paid daily as a weekly wage packet would have lost most of its value by the end of the week. The Reichsbank (State Bank) printed bank notes day and night, sometimes with quite unsuitable designs; for example in December 1922 it was intended to put a 1,000 Mark note into circulation, with the picture of a historical person engraved upon it. By the time the note was ready to go into production it had lost virtually all its value. So the Bank had printed across its front and back in large red letters: *Eine Milliarde Marks* (one thousand million Marks). When, finally, a new currency was introduced, the exchange rate was 1 New Mark = 1,000,000,000,000 Old Marks. My father, as a patriotic German, had put all his savings into Government stocks and shares. After the new currency was introduced, he received a letter from his bank saying: "Dear doctor, we have for safe keeping all your bonds and shares. If you will kindly come to this office, we shall be pleased to hand them to you. We regret that we cannot send them to you by post, since the cost of the postage stamp would exceed the value of your portfolio". So, after having worked as a doctor for twenty-five years, he had become penniless and had to start saving again when he was fifty-two years old, and a father of four children.

The financial chaos caused hardship to many professional people who were forced to look for ways of supplementing their income. I was then eleven years old, and I had recently started playing the violin. My parents wanted to find a good teacher for me. By chance, my mother had heard that one of the senior professors at the Academy of Music, who would normally only train professional musicians, was willing to give private lessons. My mother and I were received for an interview. I was rather frightened by this grumpy old man with the white beard. However he agreed to accept me as a pupil. When my mother asked him what his fee was, he replied: "There is no point in mentioning a figure. Pay me the equivalent of a loaf of bread for each lesson". Before I went for my first lesson, my mother sent me to the baker's shop in order to ask what the price of a loaf was on that day. I have forgotten the exact figure; perhaps it was 35,000 Marks. My mother put the money into an envelope and sent me off. I did not enjoy the lesson. The professor was very harsh and shouted at me: "You play like a street urchin". (To this day I have not discovered how a street urchin plays the violin.) After the lesson I handed him the envelope containing all the bank notes which would buy a loaf of bread on this day. He counted the money and after a few moments said: "Tell your mother that I am an old man and my stomach is not very good. I can only digest white bread". (This was considered to be a luxury by most people.) Fortunately, the lessons with the professor came to an end after the inflation was terminated by the introduction of a new and stable currency.

I was transferred to another teacher, Herr **Gehwald**. He was very kind and helpful and I enjoyed his lessons. For more than thirty years, Herr Gehwald was sub-leader of the orchestra of the State Opera (formerly Royal Opera) in Berlin. He possessed a beautiful Amati violin that was too precious to be taken on public transport. Therefore, he had another violin which was quite nice but much less valuable, and this violin was left permanently in the orchestra pit and he used it on all rehearsals and performances. When Herr Gehwald retired, he sold this violin to my father. I played on it for many years: it is now played by my youngest granddaughter.

Although, generally, the political atmosphere in Germany in the 1920s was gloomy, there were a few bright spots. One of these was an attempt on the part of the League of Nations to foster the reconciliation of the French and German nations by arranging an exchange of school children who would live in each other's family during the summer vacation. I had always been interested in foreign travel and I offered to take part in this exchange. The organizers of this project accepted me as a candidate; they evidently regarded me as a typical German schoolboy. They could not find the family of a

French doctor, to match my father's profession. Instead they proposed that I should accept the invitation of Monsieur **Ploussard**, a pharmacist at Châlons-sur-Marne, town in the Eastern part of France. He had a son, **Pierre**, who was fifteen years old, as I was. So one day, in the summer of 1926, I made my way into France. I interrupted the journey at Saarbrücken, where I stayed for one night with a distant relative; Saarbrücken was then a German town. On the next day I crossed into France and stopped for a few hours at Metz, a historical town which was then French, but had previously been German. After some sightseeing I wanted to go back to the railway station. I asked a man for direction to the station, in what I thought was acceptable French. However, to my shame, he answered me in German. Finally, I arrived at Châlons-sur-Marne. Monsieur Ploussard met me at the train. He was very friendly and took me to his home, which was a large and comfortable apartment situated above the pharmacy. I was introduced to the family: Madame Ploussard and their children. Pierre was their eldest child; he had a sister and a brother. Pierre had been studying German at school for some time and was keen to improve his knowledge of the language. Of course, at home only French was spoken. Madame Ploussard wanted to make sure that I should benefit as much as possible from the conversation at meal times. When she suspected that I had not understood the trend of what had been said, she called out: *"Pierre, explique!"*

Since in France the schools break up later for their summer holiday than in Germany, I accompanied Pierre to school during the first week of my visit. It was interesting for me to attend lessons in mathematics and Latin in French; but I scored a notable success in the German lesson when the teacher asked me to read aloud a poem, which I was able to do with a better accent than either he or his pupils could achieve.

During the school holidays Pierre and I made many excursions on bicycles. We explored the beautiful countryside and visited some places of historical interest. But eight years after the end of the Great War the grim reminders of the horrendous events were still visible. The battle of the Marne was one of the turning points of the

14

war, where the German army was halted and Paris was saved. But the loss of lives was enormous. We passed military cemeteries containing around twenty thousand graves; those of allied soldiers were marked by white crosses, and behind a hedge there were black crosses over the graves of German soldiers. I felt that it would take a long time for France to recover from the physical and spiritual damage inflicted upon her. Seven years later, when I was desperately looking for a country where I could find refuge from Nazi Germany, I decided that it would not be safe to go to France as it would not be strong enough to withstand Hitler's onslaught.

During my time in France Walter Jakob joined me. His aim was to find his father's grave. But this was a hopeless task. We visited several military cemeteries, each had about 20,000 graves and it was impossible to locate a particular one. On one of our final excursions we had to make a short journey by train. A French woman sat opposite us in the crowded compartment. Walter and I conversed in German. She asked us: "Are you Alsatians?" (The Alsatians are French citizens who speak a similar dialect to Swiss German.) When we told her we were Germans she hissed angrily "Boches".

My stay in France was a valuable experience. Although I was there for only five weeks, I picked up the language quite well. Pierre was a good friend. He came to live in my family for a similar period later that summer. We got on very well and his knowledge of German made good progress. After the war I got in touch with Pierre again. He had been a prisoner of war for a time, but was exchanged fairly soon with a German doctor who had been captured by the allies. Pierre's father had died and Pierre had taken over the pharmacy at Châlons-sur-Marne. Many years later, when travelling through France during our summer holiday, we stopped for a night at Châlons-sur-Marne; I was pleased to introduce Rushi and Jonathan to Pierre, who entertained us to a luxurious French dinner. Sadly, this was the last time I saw him. When we stopped again at a subsequent visit to Châlons-sur-Marne we were told that Pierre had been killed in a road accident a few weeks before.

By the 1930s the political situation had become very bad. A large part of the population had lost trust in the liberal Weimar

Republic and yearned for a drastic change. Many people, especially among the younger generation, but also some intellectuals, embraced communism in the belief that this system would eliminate unemployment and bring about a more just distribution of wealth. Others, and I think it was perhaps the majority of the German people, still bore deep resentment against the "disgraceful" peace treaty of Versailles which ended the First World War. It was indeed a fateful error on the part of some Western politicians to place humiliating conditions on Germany many years after the war. For example, as late as 1924 Germans were excluded from international meetings like the International Congress of Mathematicians. It is not surprising that many Germans gave up the hope that the 'spirit of Versailles' could be changed by peaceful means. They joined the Nazi Party because Hitler had vowed that he would restore Germany's pride. Both the communists and the Nazis wished to destroy the Weimar Republic, and to that extent, ironically, they had a common aim. I remember during a strike of the Berlin Underground Railway, two pickets guarded the entry to the Underground Station from which I normally travelled to the University. One man wore a swastika on his uniform and the other carried a red flag embossed with hammer and sickle. It was a sinister precursor of the Molotov-Ribbentrop Pact, which about seven years later gave the starting signal to the Second World War.

Despite the calamities in politics and economics, life in Berlin in the 1920s and early 1930s was not totally blighted by gloom and despondency. The flowering of the arts during that period was perhaps unsurpassed in the history of the city. Numerous theatres offered excellent performances both of the classics and of modern plays, some of which had a somewhat revolutionary tinge. Berlin has always been well supplied with museums and art galleries. I remember attending some highly illuminating lectures on classical and on modern art. But my most profound and lasting experiences were provided by the abundance and variety of first-rate musical performances which I was privileged to attend. There were three first class opera houses and the superb Berlin Philharmonic Orchestra, conducted in turn by **Wilhelm Furtwängler** and **Bruno**

Walter. Some of the most memorable recitals I attended were Arthur Schnabel's cycle of all the Beethoven Sonatas.

Initially my love of music was almost exclusively directed towards opera. My mother's father had a beautiful gramophone cabinet; its upper part contained the turntable, which had to be wound up with a handle; the lower part was reserved for the collection of records, almost all them operatic, predominately by **Richard Wagner**. My grandfather must have observed that I was fascinated when he played a record for me during one of our visits. I cannot have been more than seven years old then, because he died before I had reached the age of eight. He stipulated in his will that I should inherit the gramophone cabinet and all the records. Shortly after his death I went down with scarlet fever and had to be kept in strict isolation from the other children. But his gramophone cabinet stood by my bed and was a great consolation to me. I had asked my parents to give me the librettos of Wagner's operas. By the end of my illness I knew large parts of *Der Ring des Nibelungen* by heart.

I developed a keen interest in orchestral and choral music and when I was about twelve years old I started to play piano trios with two school friends. Our love of music brought us together, although we came from very different backgrounds. This pianist was **Ulrich Robbel**. His family included Protestant Prussian Civil Servants. Ulrich's father was manager of a Post Office. Robbel was a good musician, but he was not close to me personally. A sadistically inclined teacher tried to arouse our feeling of envy and competitiveness. He would ask me a question about classical Greek and say: "If you do not know the answer, then I shall ask Robbel". Later Robbel joined the Nazis. When, shortly before my emigration, he saw me walking near the university, he quickly crossed to the other side of the road so that he did not have to speak to me.

The cellist in our trio was **Alfons Leitl**, who was born in Austria and a devout Roman Catholic. He was not only an able cellist but also had a pleasant singing voice with which he sometimes entertained us. Leitl became a highly respected architect, specializing in the building of catholic churches. He visited us in

Sussex in 1969 and I have a number of letters from him. Sadly, he died in 1975.

It was very fortunate for me that we had a personal connection with the Berlin Philharmonic Orchestra: the porter who served this celebrated group of musicians was **Franz Jastrau**. As a boy he had been a patient of my father and he had retained a deep love and respect for his 'uncle doctor'. Jastrau had no interest in music, but he was an indispensable factotum for the members of the orchestra and he was usually allowed to claim two complimentary tickets for the 'public rehearsal' which was held on a Sunday morning, prior to the official concert by the Berlin Philharmonic Orchestra which took place on Monday evenings. Invariably Jastrau gave these two tickets to my father. My mother did not like to go out on a Sunday morning; so I had the great privilege and pleasure to attend these wonderful concerts with my father. Although they were called rehearsals, they were in fact polished performances, conducted in turn by Bruno Walter and Furtwängler. They were an invaluable part of my musical education.

I remember only one occasion that caused me disappointment and frustration. A concert had been arranged at which Rachmaninov was going to play the solo part of his latest piano concerto accompanied by the Berlin Philharmonic Orchestra conducted by Furtwängler. The tickets had been sold out for months; but Jastrau was confident that he would obtain admission for us. However, my father was unable to come, as he had to attend to a patient. So I went alone to the Philharmonic Hall and patiently waited at the agreed place near the artists' door in the hope that Furtwängler's secretary would come with the ticket. The second bell had gone and there was no sight of her. Finally she approached holding a ticket but before I could take it from her, a tall man behind me snatched it out of her hand. I looked around to see who this evildoer was and I recognized that it was Richard Strauss, who had come all the way from Bavaria to attend this concert. The concert began almost immediately. Crestfallen, I made my way home and arrived while the rest of the family were having their

Sunday lunch. My mother said: "Why are you not at the concert?" to which I replied meekly: "Richard Strauss has taken my ticket".

Opera has remained my chief interest since my adolescence. I hardly ever went to see plays at a theatre since a drama was for me simply an opera without music. The State Opera is a historical building in the centre of Berlin, maintained by the State, and was formerly called the Royal Opera House. The kings of Prussia and later, the Emperor of Germany enjoyed operatic performances there. A large space in the dress-circle was reserved for the royal visitors. In my time, the musical director of the State Opera was the eminent conductor **Erich Kleiber**. He was supported by world famous conductors, including **Leo Blech** and **Georg Szell**. My father had a season ticket for the State Opera, which provided him with two tickets for very good seats in the second circle. Sometimes, when my mother did not feel inclined to go out in the evening, my father would take me with him and we enjoyed the opera together. It was easy to get cheap tickets for the gallery. The booking office opened on Sunday morning and tickets were sold only for performances during the following week. Quite often I would take an early underground train on a Sunday morning and join the queue of opera enthusiasts and connoisseurs who were discussing the merits of the forthcoming performances before the box office opened.

I had a great passion for Wagner's music, which I shared with many people in Germany. Whist still at school there was a year during which I had heard *Die Meistersinger* fourteen times. On a certain Sunday morning I was in the queue at the box office in order to buy a ticket for *Tristan und Isolde* and met Dr **Hempel**, who taught German literature at the Leibniz Gymnasium. He asked me what opera I wanted to hear. When I told him, he asked: "How often have you heard *Tristan und Isolde*?" I said: "Four times." He replied: "I shall also buy a ticket for this opera. I have heard it one hundred and five times so far".

In the West of Berlin was the Deutsche Oper (German Opera) which was maintained by the city of Berlin. Its musical director was Bruno Walter. I remember some beautiful performances directed by him, especially operas by Mozart. Somewhat later a third opera house was established, again supported by the State of Prussia. It was situated in the centre of Berlin. It was called the Kroll Oper and its director was **Otto Klemperer**. Thus three operatic performances of the highest standard were offered every evening, except during the summer months and on the few occasions when the excellent orchestra of the opera house performed a symphony concert on the stage.

A music lover was indeed fortunate to live in Berlin in the 1920s and 1930s. It is odd that, despite their insistence on musical perfection, all operas were sung in German. As long as I lived in Germany I never heard an opera in Italian or in French. It was absurd that some of the leading singers at the State Opera like **Violetta de Strozzi** and **Tino Patiera** had to sing Puccini's operas in German. I can recall only one exception: The great Russian bass **Shaliapin** gave a small number of guest performances at the State Opera. I attended *Boris Gudenov*, in which he sang the title part magnificently in Russian while the rest of the cast harangued him in German.

My predilection for Wagner's music persisted into my student years. In 1931, after I had earned a little money by coaching school pupils, I made a 'pilgrimage' to Bayreuth. It was only two years before Hitler came to power and it was clear that a large proportion of the population supported the Nazis. There was an exaggerated veneration of Wagner throughout the little town of Bayreuth, some of it in bad taste: souvenir shops sold vessels made of red glass to represent the Holy Grail which was believed to contain the blood of Christ. Wagner's house 'Wahnfried' was open to visitors following the death of **Cosima Wagner**, who had vigorously pursued the anti-Semitic tradition of Richard Wagner. Jewish visitors were no longer denied entrance. I went into the house and saw the grand piano and the open score on it, from which Wagner requested the (Jewish) resident pianist to play to him. I also went into the garden and paid my respect at Wagner's grave. But the atmosphere was tense and rather unpleasant. My ticket was for that evening's performance of *Tannhäuser*, to be conducted by **Toscanini.**

20

However, there was a rumour going around to the effect that the performance may have to be cancelled, because at a rehearsal at that morning Toscanini had quarreled with the orchestra and declared that he would not conduct any more. But when I arrived at the Festival Theatre in the afternoon, I was told that all would be well, because **Winifred Wagner** (Richard Wagner's British daughter-in-law) had begged the maestro literally on her knees (so it was said) not to carry out his threat. Even, if he had done so, it might not have been disastrous, because Furtwängler sat behind me in the audience and would perhaps have taken over the direction. In the event it was a wonderful experience to hear Toscanini conducting the splendid orchestra, which in Bayreuth is placed underneath the stage and produces a magical sound. Unfortunately, the soloists were not all of the first class. I had heard better singing at the Berlin State Opera. On the next day I heard *Parsifal*, also beautifully conducted by Toscanini.

I did not stay on at Bayreuth. But I travelled around Bavaria for a few more days. I felt to be almost a stranger there, perhaps on account of my Berlin accent. I was amused by the beer drinking habits of the Bavarian people. When sitting down for lunch at a restaurant I was asked by the waiter not "Do you wish to have a glass of beer with your lunch, Sir?" but, "What kind of beer would you like to have with your meal?"

When I arrived at Munich I discovered that the German air line Lufthansa offered reduced fares to students at the prices of a third class rail ticket, provided that they produced a registration document from a German university. As I did not carry such a document with me, I telephoned the registry office of the university of Berlin and asked them to send by express a copy of the registration document to be collected at the main post office in Munich, which was kept open all night. The paper arrived at midnight, and I was able to claim my student ticket at the airport the next day on my return to Berlin. I was told that concession tickets would be issued only as far as the next stop on the way to Berlin, which was Leipzig, and that I would have to apply again for a ticket to the next stop. I readily agreed to this condition and was excited to become airborne, the first member of my family to fly. Unhappily, it was nearly also my last flight, because a passenger tried to commit suicide during the flight by locking himself in the lavatory and attempting to blow up the aeroplane by setting light to the fuel tank. Fortunately, the action was discovered in time by the cabin staff. The man was arrested and the plane landed safely at Leipzig and I continued my journey to Berlin.

III
The Formative Years: Berlin, 1928 – 33

I was only seventeen years of age when I left school with a Certificate of Maturity (roughly equivalent to British A-levels). This document carried with it the right of admission to any university in Germany and Austria. German students had to rely on their own financial resources to a greater extent than, for example, would be the case in modern Britain. There were few scholarships, and they were awarded only after a rigorous means test. There were no halls of residence; students lived at home or in cheap lodgings. There was no check on the attendance of lectures and, generally, no examinations before the final examination, the timing of which was determined by the candidate. Also, it was permissible to visit lectures that were not part of one's own course. One of the most agreeable privileges was the arrangement whereby a student could spend one or more semesters at different universities in Germany or Austria, and the courses he took there would be counted towards his degree.

To my mind one of the objectionable features of academic life was the arrogant and swaggering student fraternities whose members wore coloured caps and sashes. At their regular meetings they would drink inordinate amounts of beer between the renderings of noisy student songs. They were trained in sabre fencing and they were committed to fighting a duel 'in defence of their honour'. It was a matter of pride that they did not flinch when their faces were lacerated with deep cuts, which left permanent scars. Members maintained a life-long loyalty to their fraternity observing a strict hierarchy between the generations. This caused a good deal of nepotism; for example, it was said that a large proportion of the high judiciary in Germany was in the hands of the fraternities. One could see even a number of University professors with scarred faces.

The original fraternities were of some antiquity. They were fiercely nationalistic and closed to Jews. Later on, fraternities with a more liberal outlook were founded; ironically they copied the drinking habits and 'honour' code.

Fortunately, students of mathematics generally kept aloof from this snobbish sub-culture. The atmosphere in the mathematics common room was friendly, irrespective of race or religion. Such political radicalism, as existed, had a bias towards the Left, but it was always peaceful.

I was not tempted, as many students were, to spend my first semester at one of the more romantic places, like Heidelberg or Freiburg in the Black Forest. I did not seek distraction and was keen to start serious study as soon as possible. I decided to stay in Berlin and I was duly accepted as a student at the Friedrich-Wilhelms-Universität (now Humboldt Universität). To become a university student was an exhilarating experience: in some ways a university – as the name asserts – was an all-embracing *alma mater* to whom one belongs as an alumnus, and I was looking forward to the freedom and independence which was part of student life.

Among other things it was now up to me to make my own study programme by selecting suitable courses for which I wished to register. The University Office provided each student with a Study Book in which he entered the titles of all the courses he had chosen for a particular semester. (See illustration).

A small fee was paid at the Office for each course and a receipt was issued. After one of the first few lectures in the semester the student had to hand the receipt to the lecturer who in turn signed his name in the student's Study Book opposite the entry specifying the course. This procedure was known as *signing-on*. When the course involved written work that had to be marked or laboratory assignments, then the student had to present his book again at the end of the semester and ask for a second signature; this was known as *signing-off*, and it testified that the student's performance had been satisfactory. Since any check on attendance was precluded by academic freedom, it was possible for a student to be registered for a particular course by putting in a single appearance in order to sign-on and then remain absent for the remainder of the semester.

On entering the university two options were open to me: I could either seek a supervisor and work towards a doctorate, which in those days was not a postgraduate degree, or I could aim at the State Examination, which was the academic qualification for a career in the school service. I decided to adopt the second alternative, as it would offer better prospects of employment. In any event, I was not sure whether I should succeed in doing original research work.

Study Book from Friedrich-Wilhelms Universität
(highlighted, the lecture given by Prof Max Planck on 8 November 1929)

The requirements for the State Examination consisted of a high standard in two major subjects, which in my case were Mathematics and Physics, and of a more modest standard in a minor subject for which I chose Chemistry – with some hesitation because I was ill-prepared for it from school. In addition, I was also obliged to pass an oral examination in philosophy; this was due to a quirk of organization: for, although the University of Berlin was founded in the early nineteenth century, it adopted the medieval structure whereby there are only four faculties, namely Divinity, Jurisprudence, Medicine and Philosophy. As a consequence, more than half of the students belonged to the faculty of Philosophy, including students of mathematics, physics or chemistry. Moreover, there was a regulation which stipulated that every student in the faculty of Philosophy had to pass an (oral) examination in philosophy at the end of the course.

Almost all undergraduates in Berlin who studied either mathematics or physics belonged to a student society called MAPHA, which, when translated into English, stood for 'mathematical and physical study group'. The main purpose of this Society was to help one another with our studies and to get advice about our choice of lectures. There were also social events like hikes, parties and talks by outside speakers. The atmosphere was very friendly and supportive.

My widely ranging interests and obligations resulted in a heavy programme of lectures and exercise classes, amounting to more than thirty contact hours per week. On the whole, I enjoyed attending lectures even when the speaker's expository skill did not always match his fame as a scholar. But the lecturers took their tasks seriously; formally dressed, they began each lecture with "Ladies and Gentlemen". Whenever possible they tried to reach an interesting goal by the time the lecture ended after forty-five minutes.

During my fourth semester I was tempted to indulge in my love of Greek literature, and I joined a seminar in which, under the guidance of a tutor we read Plato's *Phaidros* in the original language. Although, in principle, we could choose any courses to make up the programme for a semester, there were some obvious limitations – clearly, one would not register for Analysis II without having previously attended Analysis I. Also the programme was strongly influenced by the hierarchical order within the teaching staff. At the head of each branch of the subject was the 'Ordinarius', that is Full Professor. Only an Ordinarius was in receipt of a salary, which presumably was quite generous; in fact, he was a Civil Servant with permanent tenure and entitlement to a pension. Undergraduates were not normally allowed to approach an Ordinarius unless they had previously spoken to one of his Assistants. The Ordinarius representing the subject gave all the important courses. Next in the academic hierarchy came the Extra-Ordinarius (Associate

Professor). He would occasionally obtain a contract to give certain lecture courses; but his position was inferior to that of an Ordinarius. At the bottom of the ladder was the Privat-Dozent (Private Lecturer). His remuneration consisted solely of the modest fees paid by the students attending his class. Quite often the courses offered by a Private Dozent were on specialized topics and attracted only a small number of students. Thus the income was minimal; indeed, it would appear that under the prevailing system only a person of private means or outside income could embark on an academic career.

Erhard Schmidt

Most of the mathematicians whose lectures I attended made a lasting impression on me, and I still have vivid memories of them even after seventy years. **Erhard Schmidt** was the Ordinarius for Analysis. Before coming to Berlin he had done brilliant work at Göttingen, and he enjoyed a world-wide reputation. He was a man of impressive appearance and charismatic personality, but he seemed utterly unapproachable to me. During the four semesters when I attended his lectures I never dared to address a word to him, and he took no notice of me. There was an air of improvisation in the way he delivered his lectures; indeed, one had the feeling that he was rediscovering the most intricate mathematical results on the spur of the moment. He despised learning by rote. His advice was: "Never try to memorize a formula. Either it represents an important fact; then you will meet it in your studies so often that you will not forget it, or it is not an important formula. Then there is no reason why you should remember it."

Surprisingly, Erhard Schmidt could be funny; in fact, he possessed considerable histrionic talents. He was of Baltic origin, and he spoke German with a heavy drawl, typical of his native dialect. I suppose this feature made his jocular remarks all the more amusing. He began his first lecture with the words: "Ladies and Gentlemen, for the sake of brevity allow me to address you all henceforth as Gentlemen". Often, there were visiting students from other faculties who sat giggling at the back of the classroom. They had come to be entertained by this eccentric professor of mathematics, although they could not understand one word of what he said. It seemed that Erhard Schmidt had numerous evening engagements outside the university. He therefore found it convenient to give his lectures from 6 p.m. till 8 p.m. because the venues of his appointments could be more readily reached from the university, which was situated in the centre of the city, than from his home on the outskirts. Sometimes he came to his lecture wearing a dress suit and the porter came to the classroom at 8 p.m. and said:" Sir, your taxi is outside".

The difficulties which many students may have had with the intellectual challenge of Erhard Schmidt's lectures were mitigated by the invaluable help provided by Dr. **Georg Feigl.** He was an Assistant to Erhard Schmidt. Feigl's course *Introduction to Higher Mathematics* was an outstanding achievement in academic teaching. It eased for us the transition from school to university and filled the gaps in our understanding of some of the difficult parts of Erhard Schmidt's lectures. Feigl also conducted exercise classes for Erhard Schmidt's course on Analysis. Evidently, the grand man eschewed the lowly task of setting weekly exercises, let alone marking them. Feigl was also a lecturer in his own right. I remember his course on Projective Geometry which was so popular that it had to be held in the Auditorium Maximum of the University. But there was such a heavy demand on this hall that the only slot that could be found for Feigl and his audience, to which I belonged, was from 7.15 a.m. till 9 a.m. on two days of the week. This situation, coupled with Erhard Schmidt's propensity to evening lectures made it necessary for me to spend 13 hours in the university on certain days, to which had to be added one hours journey from and to my home.

The person who had by far the strongest influence on my career was **Issai Schur**, the Ordinarius for Algebra. He was a superb lecturer. His courses were extremely well structured and organized: they were divided into chapters and subsection, each with a separate number. He prepared his lectures so well that he delivered them without recourse to the notes, which, as I learned later, he carried in the pocket of his jacket. Schur's lectures were very popular. His introductory courses on algebra were attended by about 300 students. On some days I was able only to secure a seat in one of the back rows and had to use opera glasses in order to read his writing on the black board.

I felt that Schur's lectures were perfect in form and content. I took rough notes of what he said during the lectures and later, during week-ends or vacations, I transcribed them into cloth-bound books. They comprise some 2000 pages of about 320 lectures given by Schur on various branches of algebra and number theory. I greatly treasured these hand-written books as a monument of Schur's supreme knowledge and wisdom and I frequently referred to them throughout my career. Finally, in 1998 I donated the books to the Humboldt University, the name now given to the Friedrich-Wilhelms University where I was a student from 1928 till 1933.

Schur was born in Russia. But he was educated at a German-speaking school and he spoke German so well that one could not detect that German was not his native language. He was Jewish and when the Nazis came to power in 1933 he was immediately dismissed and forbidden to enter the university. Just before the catastrophe I had registered as a candidate for the Final Examination and I had the good fortune that Schur agreed to supervise my dissertation. As I could no longer see him in his office at the university he kindly invited me to his home at the outskirts of Berlin in order to discuss my work. On these occasions, after we had finished our mathematical business, we shared our deep anxieties about the fate that would befall the Jews under the Nazi tyranny. Schur said: "I find it too distasteful to read German newspapers, as they have all been taken over by the Nazis. It is a blessing that the London *Times* is still obtainable here, which enables me to keep in touch with the world."

For six years Schur and his wife endured harassment and persecution at the hands of the Nazis. Several of his former students, who had found refuge in Britain, tried to persuade Schur to join them; but he declined giving as one of his reasons that he was reluctant to change his language again. Finally, he was able to go to Switzerland, where his daughter lived. From there he reached Palestine. By then he was a broken man in spirit and body. He died in 1941 on his 66th birthday.

The third Ordinarius for pure mathematics was **Ludwig Bieberbach**. He was an eminent mathematician and the author of several useful textbooks. But he was a poor lecturer. I remember him nervously flitting through the pages of a copy of his own book, which lay in front of him, in order to find some help in continuing the argument he tried to expound in the lecture. Bieberbach disgraced himself by being one of the (happily few) German mathematicians who became active Nazis.

Shortly after Hitler's accession to power Bieberbach strutted along the corridors of the University proudly sporting a brown uniform. He pushed racial doctrines to absurd limits by founding the journal *Deutsche Mathematik* (German Mathematics) in which only authors of Nordic blood were allowed to publish, and he asserted that their mathematical work was superior to that produced by authors of Latin or Jewish 'race'. I have not seen Bieberbach's journal, but I remember reading a review by G.H. Hardy, which ended somewhat as follows: "In times of political upheaval we may occasionally make statements that we do not really mean and later regret. But in the case of Bieberbach I have come to the less charitable conclusion that he believes what he says."

The Ordinarius for Applied Mathematics was **Richard von Mises**, an Austrian nobleman of Jewish extraction. The field of his interests and creative contributions was very wide; it included most branches of mathematics, engineering, aviation, philosophy and literature, especially the work of the poet Rainer Maria Rilke. Mises was very sure of himself. He spoke and wrote with precision and authority and with an aristocratic demeanour. After the lecture an assistant stood behind the door, holding a brush. Ready to remove any speck of dust that might have settled on the master's well-cut suit.

In those days, Applied Mathematics included not only Mechanics, but also Geometric Drawing, Numerical Analysis (before the existence of electronic computers!), Probability Theory and Statistics. I vividly remember his course on Probability, in which he expounded his original definition of randomness. I thought it was a brilliant idea, and I regretted that it was not more widely accepted. This was in 1931, the year in which he published his substantial treatise *Wahrscheinlichkeitrechnung* (Calculus of Probability). This was intended to be the first of a series of volumes on various topics in applied mathematics. Alas, it was not to be: for, being of Jewish origin, Mises was dismissed from his post by the Nazis. He accepted a position in Istanbul (which, however, he soon left in order to go to America). At that time I was anxiously looking for a country to which I could escape from the Nazis. In my admiration of Mises I took the bold step of telephoning him at home and said: "Professor, please excuse my intrusion. I understand that you are going to Istanbul. Would you be willing to accept me as a student, and could I study for a doctorate at Istanbul?". His typically curt reply was: "Of course, you can take a doctorate anywhere".

I also attended some courses given by junior members of the faculty, that is by lecturers who were not an Ordinarius. Among these, the person who had the strongest influence on me was Dr. **Heinz Hopf**. Already before 1930 he had gained a high reputation through his fundamental contribution to algebraic topology, and it was not surprising that in 1931 he was offered a post of Ordinarius at the prestigious Swiss Federal Institute of Technology (ETH) in Zürich, where he remained for the rest of his life. It was fortunate for me that Hopf was still in Berlin during most of my student years. I was fascinated by his lectures on Topology that he gave in 1930. It was then a new subject and rarely included in the undergraduate syllabus. Even more important for my mathematical education was the fact that in 1929 Hopf gave the main course on Functions of a Complex Variable. Normally, this course would have been given by the Ordinarius, that is by Erhard Schmidt. But in 1929 Schmidt had been elected to be the Rector (RECTOR MAGNIFICUS) of the University and he found it necessary to reduce his teaching commitments. So he asked Heinz Hopf to take over this course. Hopf carried out his task in a masterly fashion. His lectures were meticulously prepared and he delivered them in a clear voice and with excellent black board technique. The course was spread over two semesters. It began with very simple material, explaining even what a complex number was. But at the end of the second semester he introduced us to some deep results concerning the geometric aspect of function theory.

Heinz Hopf

Hopf left Berlin to take up his post at Zürich, and I did not see him for a further fifteen years. In the meantime, I had settled in Great Britain and the world was beginning to recover from the horrors of Hitler's war. I married after the war and my wife's parents lived in Zürich, where her father was a professor of the History of Art. We often had an opportunity of traveling to Zürich to visit her parents. On these occasions I would call on Hopf, who kindly invited me to his house and sometimes went for a walk with me. He spoke to me about his years in Berlin when I was his student. One of the outstanding events in the history of algebra was the publication of van der Waerden's book *Moderne Algebra*, which brought about a strong tendency towards abstraction. Some of the younger members of the Faculty, including Hopf, thought it would be a good idea to hold a weekly seminar in which van der Waerden's book could be studied by all the members. But the academic etiquette in those days required that such a seminar could take place only with the permission of Issai Schur, who was the Professor of Algebra. There was a belief that Schur did not like abstract algebra and might therefore not approve of this seminar. So, Hopf's colleagues said to him: "You are polite and well dressed (which some of the others were not), go to Schur on our behalf and ask him for permission to run the seminar." Hopf had an interview with Schur, who readily gave his approval but added: "I shall not take part." Hopf was pleased that he had the opportunity to give the course on Complex Variables, and, in particular, that so many students attended it. "I used the fees for it to pay for my honeymoon", he told me.

Heinz Hopf visited the United Kingdom a few times. He was once the main speaker at a meeting of the British Mathematical Colloquium. After the meeting he was the guest at one of the Cambridge Colleges, I think it was Trinity. He dined at High Table; the don who sat next to him was not a mathematician but he tried to involve the distinguished foreign visitor in conversation. He asked: "Are you a Trinity man?" When Hopf replied: "No", he continued: "Where you at St. Johns?" When the answer was again, "no", his host went through another ten or so Colleges. Hopf got more and more puzzled but kept up his denials. Then there was a pause and Hopf hoped that the topic of the conversation would be changed. However, his neighbour now declared with conviction: "So you were at Oxford."

The study of physics, which was the second subject for my State Diploma, was less enjoyable for me than my involvement with mathematics. This was partly due to the fact that I had very little teaching of physics at school, but also because I felt that I had no talent for science. However, there was some incentive for pursuing my work in physics: at that time there were some famous physicists in Berlin, and I was curious to see them and to listen to their lectures. Most of the material contained in the remainder of this chapter was published in an article *Physics in Berlin 1928-33*, (Physics Bull. 38 (1987) (IOP Publishing Ltd.). I should like to thank the Editor for giving permission to reproduce the article here, with minor alterations.

In the first year, for two semesters, students of physics were expected to attend the course on experimental physics given by **Walther Nernst**. He was a colourful person. Originally a professor of Chemistry – he had been awarded the Nobel Prize for chemistry – he became a professor of Physical Chemistry, a subject for which he had laid the foundation through his celebrated textbook. Finally, he was appointed to the professorship in Physics. He was fond of remarking that he was a successor both to Bunsen and to Helmholtz. To us undergraduates he seemed arrogant, pompous and unapproachable. Nevertheless, ironically, he addressed the students by the egalitarian term of *"commilitones"* (fellow soldiers).

His lectures were unsystematic and difficult to follow. The vast majority of students who had to register for his course stayed away after a single attendance when they handed over their vouchers for the fee paid and obtained Nernst's signature in their study book. But on the first few days of the semester the lecture theatre was overcrowded with many students sitting on the steps or standing. Nernst came into the class room and said amiably: "Dear commilitones, I am so sorry about the inconvenience so many are being put to because of the lack of seating accommodation. But I can assure you that there will be plenty of empty seats in a week from now." He was right. For the rest of the semester the lecture theatre was half empty. But I persisted with my attendance. Although his talent for communication was modest, I could sense that I was in the presence of a great scientist who had a deep insight into the laws of nature.

His vanity could also lead to amusing incidents. One of these occurred when he wanted to demonstrate that a difference of electrical potential will arise when a disc of base metal touches a disc of gold. He told us that many years ago this experiment was shown to an audience of wealthy amateurs of science. The lecturer produced an iron disc and then said: "Gentlemen, I should be obliged if one of you could lend me a gold coin so that I can continue with the experiment." The request was immediately granted, several outstretched arms offering purses filled with gold sovereigns. Now Nernst turned to us: "Dear commilitones, I do not expect that any one of you could lend me a gold coin at this moment. So I have taken the precaution of bringing some of my own collection. He clapped his hands and the laboratory technician came in carrying a tray covered with a velvet cloth, on which lay a number of gold medals. Nernst picked them up one by one making such comments as, "This is the Nobel Prize. This is the Bunsen Medal, this is the Franklin Medal", and with audible aside: "as far as I know there is one other such medal in Europe; it belonged to my friend the late Herr Boltzmann in Vienna", and so on. It was a most effective performance despite its boastfulness and conceit.

When I started my course, the Ordinarius for Theoretical Physics was **Max Planck**. His personality was very different from that of Nernst. Planck was quiet-spoken and reticent about his achievements. He always wore a black frock-coat, old-fashioned even in the 1920s. He taught theoretical physics in a cycle of five one-semester courses, comprising general mechanics, mechanics of continua, electricity and magnetism, optics and thermodynamics. In the winter of 1929 it was once again the turn of thermodynamics, and there was a rumour that Planck would retire after completing this cycle.

Max Plank

I was anxious not to miss the opportunity of having been a student of Max Planck, so I registered for the thermodynamics course although I was not really ready for it, because I had not attended the preceding four courses. There were several hundred students in his class. After one of the first few lectures we queued in order to hand in our vouchers and to obtain Planck's signature in our Study Books. He dealt rapidly with the waiting students. But when my turn came, he paused and said to me: "If you have any difficulties with my lectures, do not hesitate to come to my office. I shall be very pleased to answer your questions if I can". I was very touched by his encouragement; perhaps he felt that I needed it, because I was the youngest student in the class. However, I never accepted his invitation.

Planck's lectures were well prepared and, as one would expect of high intellectual standard. To be sure, his mathematics was a little old-fashioned and did not always conform to the rigour that was demanded in our pure mathematics courses. Regrettably, the effectiveness of his lectures was diminished by an unfortunate blackboard technique: before each lecture the porter brought a sponge and a saucer filled with water. Planck carefully squeezed the sponge until it was thoroughly moist. He held the sponge in his left hand while rapidly writing on the board with his right hand. Then, after covering a few lines he deleted everything with a sudden swing of his left arm. Thus it was difficult to take notes unless you were sitting at the extreme right of the room.

Apparently, Planck was too senior or too old to undertake the labour of holding the exercise classes that supplemented his course on Thermodynamics. So this task was delegated to **Max von Laue**, himself a Nobel Laureate. Von Laue had a slight speech defect and did not enjoy lecturing to young students. His exercise class was offered as a *collegium publicum*; no fee was payable and we did not get his signature in our Study Books. Von Laue's problems were very hard, and I did not succeed in solving many of them, but neither did the other students. He gave us the solutions of those questions from the preceding week which nobody had been able to solve Then he addressed us in his staccato voice: "Are there any questions? If not, then I will close for to-day", and the class was dismissed after about 25 minutes.

As had been anticipated, Planck retired on completion of his course on Thermodynamics. His successor was **Erwin Schrödinger**. He was very different from the professors I had encountered so far. When he came to Berlin, he was in his mid-forties, a good-looking man with a scintillating personality. For many of us his charm was enhanced by an attractive Austrian accent. He was lively and informal. On a summer's day he would come to his lecture in an open-neck shirt, an attire utterly alien to a Prussian professor. Once, he was stopped by the security guard who thought he was a political agitator; one of his students had to arrange for his release, because Schrödinger carried no identity papers.

His lectures were well thought out but delivered in a somewhat improvised manner. He did not adopt Planck's five-semester cycle of clearly defined topics, but he divided the subject into field physics and corpuscular physics, devoting two semesters to each. Schrödinger had a complete mastery of mathematical techniques and a deep insight into mathematical ideas and principles. But his mathematics was always related to the physical theories which it served to describe. He once said: "I am often asked for advice about the best way to study theoretical physics. My reply is: In the first year you study only mathematics; in the second year you study only mathematics. In the third year you can come to me, and we shall talk about physics."

Despite his great intellectual power Schrödinger had retained an endearing boyish trait. One day, a Zeppelin was flying over Berlin and could be seen from the University. When he noticed this, he ran to the window of the classroom and shouted: "Look at the Zeppelin".

When the Nazis came to power in March 1933 Schrödinger had been in his position only for a few years. Yet in the summer of 1933 he suddenly left and never returned to Berlin. He was not Jewish and his departure had nothing to do with the Nazi racial laws. I was given the following explanation of this extraordinary event: one of the first things Hitler tried to do was to coerce Austria by economic means and in particular to destroy Austria's tourist industry. So he decreed that German citizens who wished to travel to Austria would have to pay a fee of 1000 Mark for an exit visa. This was a very large sum of money and virtually stopped all travelling from Germany to Austria. As was his custom, Schrödinger wanted to spend the summer holiday in his native country. So he applied to the Nazi authorities for exemption from the prohibitive travel tax. But his request was refused on the grounds that he was now a German citizen after having accepted the appointment as a Full Professor at a German university. Schrödinger was very angry. Instead of going to Austria he went to Oxford, where, I am sure, he was well received. From there he sent a postcard to the head porter of the University of Berlin who had the (rather funny) name Pfannkuchen (Pancake) saying: "Dear Herr Pfannkuchen, please tell the Senate that I am not coming back" This was, of course, regarded as a deliberate insult by the Nazi authorities who swore that they would severely punish Schrödinger, whenever they could lay hands on him.

In 1936 the Chair of Natural Philosophy (Physics) in Edinburgh became vacant. **Whittaker** thought that Schrödinger might be interested in the position; but he added: "It would be inappropriate to have a man of such distinction interviewed by a panel. So, I will explain to him personally what the appointment would entail". Schrödinger was invited to come to Edinburgh and Whittaker met him at Waverley Station. I may mention that Whittaker was always dressed in a conventional manner: dark suit and coat, hat and, of course, carrying an umbrella. On the next day he gave us an account of his meeting with Schrödinger. "I suggested that we walk around Arthur's Seat while I would describe to him the duties of an Edinburgh professor. Then it started to rain, and, would you believe it, Professor Schrödinger pulled out of his pocket a close-fitting arrangement that he proceeded to put on his head". It was clear that for this and, no doubt, weightier reasons, Whittaker came to the conclusion that Schrödinger would not be happy with a position in Edinburgh. Shortly afterwards Schrödinger accepted an invitation to join the Institute for Advanced Study in Dublin, in which President de Valera took a personal interest (he had mathematical training). It is possible that Whittaker had something to do with this appointment because he had been on friendly terms with de Valera since the time when he was Astronomer Royal of Ireland, before moving to Edinburgh in 1912.

Schrödinger's enmity towards the Nazis nearly had disastrous consequences for him. He was in Austria in 1938 when the Nazis invaded that country. They had not forgotten the insult he had inflicted on them in 1933. He was arrested and deprived of his freedom to travel abroad. But Schrödinger was too clever for them. He pretended that he had been converted to the Nazi ideology and he issued an open declaration expressing regret that he had misunderstood the great German revival and that he would now gladly join the ranks of his Aryan compatriots. His insult of 1933 was forgiven. Unhindered he slipped out of the country and went back to Ireland, where he spent the rest of his working life. In his old age he returned to Austria, and he died there in 1961.

Albert Einstein's Research Institute was situated near Berlin. As he was also a member of the Prussian Academy, he was automatically associated with the University. But as far as I know he gave no under-graduate courses in my time. However, it was our ambition to have Einstein as a speaker at one of our Mapha (Mathematica Arbeitsgemeinschaft – Mathematical workshop) meetings. This proved to be difficult to arrange, because Mrs. Einstein always answered the door and prevented any caller from approaching her husband. However, some students had noticed that during the summer Einstein often worked in the roof garden of his villa near Berlin. So, two representatives from Mapha climbed up the drainpipe and appeared on the wall of the garden. Somewhat taken aback by the intrusion Einstein asked: "What do you want", and one of the students replied: "Professor, please forgive the disturbance; but would you be willing to give a lecture for the Mapha?" Einstein consented and a date was fixed. The lecture was, in fact, open to all members of the University, who filled the Auditorium Maximum to capacity. He presented a popular and fascinating account of the General Theory of Relativity.

My Oral Examination for the State Examination took place in November 1933, when the Nazis had been in power for eight months. The political revolution cast its shadows even on purely academic pursuits. Candidates were allowed to express a wish as to who should be their examiner in any particular subject. I had a difficulty in choosing an examiner for Philosophy. I was told that all the professors of philosophy at the university were Nazi sympathizers and would probably fail me because I was a Jew. Then somebody mentioned that **Professor Metzner** was a member of the examination board although he was on the staff of the Technical University. It was known that the Professor was a devout Roman Catholic. At that time, the Catholic Zentrum Party did not support Hitler. Some months before the examination was to be held I asked Professor Metzner for an interview. I told him that I was a mathematician and had also attended a course on mathematical logic. He accepted me as a candidate and gave me some reading to do. On the morning of the oral examination Professor Metzner was delayed. When he finally arrived he was flustered but apologetic. I was the first candidate. He said: "I know you are a mathematician. Would you say that mathematical logic has invalidated the classical work of Aristotle?" I knew what was in his mind. Aristotelian philosophy has played an important part in Catholic theology, and he was afraid that the mathematical approach had undermined catholic teaching. I replied:" Mathematics offers a new approach to logic; but it has not diminished the importance of Aristotle's work". He was obviously pleased and said: "This is what I have always said. I'll give you Grade A - Next candidate, please!"

It was very fortunate that the examination in mathematics could proceed as planned. Schur, who had been dismissed in March of that year, was temporarily reinstated through the intervention of his colleague Erhard Schmidt and was therefore able to conduct the examination. The co-examiner, that is the person who acted as a secretary for the proceedings, was Ludwig Bieberbach. This was unpleasant for Schur and for me, for Bieberbach was an enthusiastic Nazi and appeared wearing his brown uniform. However, it should be said that he did not interfere in any hostile manner. I still remember Schur's first question: "What, in your opinion, is the most important theorem of the differential calculus?" I said: "Taylor's Theorem", and he replied: "I disagree. Surely, once you have proved Rolle's Theorem, the other main theorems can easily be deduced from it". He then went on to algebra. "How do you determine the rank of a matrix?" Passing to complex analysis, he asked "What is the addition theorem for the Weierstrass elliptic function?" I started to recall the rather complicated formula; but I got stuck and had to admit that I did not remember the last term in the denominator. After a few seconds Schur said: "I don't remember it either". It was then that Bieberbach spoke, the only time during the examination; without hesitation he quoted the complete formula. Schur was pleased that I could cite various details in the theory of conformal mappings. "How is it that you know all this?" he asked, and I replied: "I learned it in Dr. Hopf's lectures." Schur had put me at my ease, and the Oral Examination, which I had feared would be an awful ordeal, turned out to be quite a pleasant experience.

This concluded my life as a mathematician in Berlin. I was soon to leave my native city. More than forty years elapsed before I saw Berlin again, when I accompanied my wife on a professional meeting that was held in that city. However, I gratefully remember the foundations for my career that I received from the University of Berlin and the enriching experiences I had when the cultural life of Berlin was at its peak.

IV
Emigration: St. Andrews, 1934 – 36

From the outset it was clear to me that I should have no chance of surviving in Nazi Germany. I made strenuous efforts to emigrate. Eventually, owing to a chance remark my brother had overheard in Edinburgh, I obtained a scholarship through the good offices of the International Student Service at Geneva: the students at St. Andrews University had decided to support two refugees from Nazi Germany, one who was persecuted on account of his political affiliations and the other because he was Jewish. It was my exceedingly good fortune that I was selected for the second award. I understood later that the money for our maintenance had been collected from the citizens and students of St. Andrews. Indeed, it is no exaggeration to affirm that I owe my life to the people of St. Andrews.

I vividly remember the circumstances of my emigration. I was due to leave on 3rd January 1934. It was my wish to spend my last evening at the opera. My father obtained two tickets for a performance of *Tristan und Isolde* at the State Opera House, Unter den Linden. This being a long opera, the performance was scheduled to start at 7 p.m. Normally the timing was strictly adhered to; but on that evening the lights did not go out at 7 p.m. and it was clear that something unusual was happening. Then, when all members of the audience were in their seats, we saw there was some movement in the Grand Imperial box, in the centre of the Dress Circle. Adolph Hitler came in; he was wearing a dinner jacket. A young lady accompanied him. They sat down in the first row and were followed by Goebbels and a woman who took seats behind Hitler. But the lights still did not go out. We then observed that Goering had come in wearing his uniform with numerous medals. He did not sit with Hitler but occupied a box in the second circle quite near where my father and I were sitting. Then, finally, the performance began. It was beautifully done, Furtwängler conducted. As always, the orchestra played superbly and there was a first class cast of soloists. The role of King Marke was sung by the excellent

44

bass Emmanuel List, who was Jewish (perhaps this was kept from Hitler so as not to spoil his enjoyment). For me it was an ideal way to be granted this musical treat on my last evening in Germany, although I had to share it with Hitler, Goebbels and Goering.

I left the next morning. My parents could not see me off, as it was a working day for my father. But my sister Käte came with me to the Bahnhof Friederichstrasse and waved good-bye as the train left for Holland. I was destined not to see her again for almost twenty years. My plan was to go first to Edinburgh, where my brother Erich was working in order to obtain a British medical qualification, and then to go on to St. Andrews two days later.

The third class compartment in which I was travelling was fully occupied. Nobody spoke to me. The first stop was Hanover. I was horrified when two SS soldiers in black uniform stormed into our compartment and seized two middle-aged men and pulled them out of the train. As the train was beginning to move out of the station we threw the men's suitcases out of the window. I have no idea why these men were arrested. Perhaps they were trying to smuggle money out of Germany. The frightening thought occurred to me that one of the passengers in our compartment was a Nazi spy who communicated with the police and had informed them of the men's location. Not another word was spoken until we had crossed the Dutch border. Everybody's face brightened up with relief that at last we had reached freedom.

The train took us to Hook-van-Holland, where I boarded the boat to Harwich. On arrival at Harwich I saw several trains at the quayside; one was clearly marked 'Edinburgh', and I quickly got into it with my luggage. The train left and a few minutes later the ticket collector came. When he looked at my ticket, it became clear that I was on the wrong train. I should have gone to London and then taken the 'Flying Scotsman' from Kings Cross Station to Edinburgh. My heart sank because I felt sure that I should have to buy the correct ticket for this train. To my surprise the collector just waved his hand and said: "Never mind! It is the wrong ticket; but continue your journey to Edinburgh." It was my first encounter with a pleasant British characteristic: absence of rigid bureaucracy and a sense of humour.

Having travelled throughout the night I was hungry and sat down in the attractive dining car and studied the menu. A nice Dutch gentleman sat at the same table; he spoke English and German and he explained to me that full English breakfast includes bacon and eggs. This was new to me. I ordered it and I enjoyed it - the second encounter with a pleasant British custom. When I arrived in Edinburgh, I was very pleased to see Erich at the platform. Luckily he had made enquiries and been told that the 'wrong' train I had taken was the official boat train. I spent two pleasant days in Edinburgh and then continued my journey to St Andrews.

On my arrival, **William (Bill) McC. Stewart**, the local representative of the International Student Service met me. Stewart was the Head of the French Department at St. Andrews. Bill was a lively and cultured Ulsterman. Apart from being fluent in French he had an excellent command of German, so that I had no difficulty in communicating with him. He had recently married a Jewish lawyer from Munich, so I felt very much at home with the Stewarts, who lived in one of the few modern houses of St. Andrews. Bill Stewart remained my mentor and friend for many years to come and I was most grateful to him. He introduced me to **D.E. (Dan) Rutherford** who was one of the three lecturers in the Mathematics Department. Dan spoke some German, as he had spent one semester at Göttingen as a postgraduate student. My friendship with Dan was most precious to me. Coming as he did, from a background very different from my own, he greatly enriched my life. He also helped me in a practical way to settle down in the new surroundings.

I could read English fairly well, but the spoken language caused considerable difficulty. I tried to improve my vocabulary. One method was to walk through the streets of St. Andrews in order to learn words from inscriptions on shops and notice boards. I had no problem with 'Tobacconist' or 'Newsagent'. I understood the meaning of 'Fishmonger' after looking up the second part of the word in a dictionary; but a 'Family Butcher' was to my mind an outrageously cruel occupation. However, I settled down fairly rapidly in these very strange surroundings. The terms of the scholarship laid it down that I should receive a sum of money (if I remember rightly, £5 per week) to cover the cost of lodgings and breakfast.

Dan Rutherford

My landlady was a simple-minded elderly woman who was sometimes slightly the worse for drink. She had four male students in her flat, which was part of an old house in the centre of St. Andrews. There was no electricity in the house. We were each given a box containing three matches with which we could turn on the gas light when we came home after dark. She explained that she was unwilling to give us a full match box as we might use the matches to light our cigarettes or pipes. But she was prepared to issue three more matches when asked to do so. The lack of electricity puzzled me, especially when I discovered that there were some quite modern cottages without this service. Then it was explained to me that the chairman of the local gas company (which at that time was privately owned) was also an influential member of the town council and he used his influence to withhold planning permission from any building that was planning to have electricity installed.

I was the guest of the Students Union for lunch in their dining room. For the evening meal I joined the students at St. Salvator's Hall. This was the main Hall of Residence for male students. It was a spacious and fairly modern building. The rules of conduct were in the Oxford and Cambridge style. Dinner was 'formal', that is, the Warden and other members of faculty sat at the High Table; they wore black gowns. The students sat at long tables below the High Table. They had to wear the scarlet gown which was characteristic for St. Andrews. Fortunately, Erich knew a lady in Edinburgh who had been a student at St. Andrews and kindly passed her scarlet gown on to me.

These arrangements made it easy for me to mix with other students. Most of them were from Scotland, a few from England, but only a small number from other countries. Some of the students I met were studying German as a foreign language. We helped each other with our linguistic endeavours by going for walks along the beach speaking German on the way out and English on the way back, or *vice versa*. There were also some faculty members, rather more often their wives, who wanted to brush up their conversational German. Usually they invited me to tea and we had a conversation in German afterwards.

Another way to meet people was through music. I had my violin and viola with me. Soon I found pianists who played sonatas with me and I took part in the annual performance of *The Messiah* by a capable amateur choir and orchestra. As in most universities, St. Andrews students had their 'hop' on Saturday evenings. Regrettably, I had never succeeded in learning ballroom or folk dancing. But I offered to bring my violin and to play Scottish Reels and Strathspeys while the rest of the company enjoyed itself on the dance floor. Other social occasions to play music were the meetings of the Franco-Scottish Society, which was founded to commemorate the alliance in former times between France and Scotland in their fight against England. At these meetings only French was spoken and French music was performed. I was invited as a guest and to play pieces by Couperin and Rameau.

Initially, there was uncertainty about my status at the University. It was my hope that I should be allowed to work for a doctorate. But since this is a higher degree, candidates must have a first degree before being admitted. The question was whether the State Examination from Berlin could be regarded as equivalent to a

British B.Sc. degree. This problem had never occurred in the five hundred year history of St. Andrews University. Fortunately, it was discovered that a similar case had recently been considered in Edinburgh. A refugee had arrived with complete teaching qualification and she was given permission to register for a Ph.D. degree. (In fact, this individual was **Charlotte Auerbach**, who became an eminent geneticist in Edinburgh and was one of the few women to be elected to a Fellowship of the Royal Society of London.)

I was very pleased that Professor **H.W. Turnbull**, the (only) Professor of Mathematics at that time, accepted me as one of his research students. He was a well-known authority on classical algebra, which had been my favourite subject as an undergraduate. I was particularly interested in his joint book with A.C. Aitken on *Canonical Matrices*, a brilliant work that suggested areas for further research. Professor Turnbull was a patient and understanding supervisor. Before being appointed to the Regius Chair of Mathematics at St. Andrews he had spent several years as a missionary in China and had acquired some knowledge of the Chinese language. During one of our early sessions, Professor Turnbull noticed that I was struggling with words and he kindly said to me: "Walter, I see that you have difficulties in expressing yourself; would it help you if I spoke to you in Chinese?" I politely declined adding that I would prefer to stick to English, however imperfect on my part.

It is hard to imagine a greater difference than between Berlin and St. Andrews. Life in a large city can be impersonal and may lead to a sense of isolation. But in a small town like St. Andrews I soon got to know almost everybody – at least by sight. I was frequently invited, usually for tea, and I was always received with warm hospitality. Professor and Mrs. Turnbull were particularly caring and helpful. In the warm season they often asked me to join them for a picnic. (It is unlikely that a German professor would do this with one of his doctoral candidates.)

Herbert Turnbull

I observed that, in general, religion played a more prominent part in the lives of the British people than was the case in comparable continental communities. Both Professor Turnbull and Dan Rutherford were devout Christians. Indeed Professor Turnbull usually began his lecture with a prayer. He and Mrs. Turnbull belonged to the Oxford Group, a religious movement, which had gained some influence in the 1930s. Occasionally they held meetings at their house for members of this group. After partaking of an enjoyable afternoon tea, the participants would sit in a circle and 'with perfect honesty' would publicly confess their misdeeds or sinful thoughts. I had been invited to several of these meetings but felt increasingly uncomfortable. Eventually, I appealed to the principle of 'perfect honesty' and confessed that I would prefer not to be asked to attend any more meetings of the Oxford Group.

Both Professor and Mrs. Turnbull were excellent pianists. Quite often, after a delicious tea they played to me works on two pianos; for example the St. Anthony Variations by Brahms and the work better known as Piano Quintet by Brahms, but originally scored for two pianos. Much later my memory of these splendid pieces of music was revived after my marriage to Rushi; she played them with our friends; for although at the beginning of our marriage we had rather modest houses, we made sure that there was always enough room for two pianos in our music room.

Mountaineering was another of Professor Turnbull's hobbies. I was told that one tricky route to the top of a particular mountain in the Scottish Highlands was named after him, because he was the first to have reached the peak in this way. He had frequently undertaken major mountaineering expeditions in Switzerland, including an ascent of the Matterhorn with the aid of a professional guide. Surprisingly, St. Andrews offered opportunities for practising one's mountaineering skill, albeit on a small scale. Turnbull was particularly fond of a rock formation called the Rock and Spindle. It was situated on the Eastern shore of St. Andrews. Turnbull would take his students to this place and give them some experience in rock climbing. One day he took me to this impressive place. At low tide the rock could be reached on foot; but at high tide it was completely surrounded by the sea. We started our climb at low tide. Under his guidance I managed to reach the top albeit rather slowly. I was rather worried lest the tide might come back before I got down and I said: "Professor Turnbull, what shall I do if the tide has come in before I have completed the descent?" He answered rather typically: "Then you will just have to pray." Fortunately, this was not necessary, as I got down in time.

The rest on Sunday (or the "Sabbath Day" as some Scots say) was strictly observed and even enforced by law. There were no trains or buses operating at St. Andrews on a Sunday. Cinemas were closed, and restaurants were open only for a few hours. Most students attended University Chapel. One Sunday after the other lodgers had left and I stayed behind, the landlady said to me; "why don't you go to church"? I replied: "Because I am Jewish". "That does not matter", she said. "We have churches for Presbyterians, Anglicans, Methodists and others; surely, one of them will suit you." After Chapel, the students, wearing their bright scarlet gowns would walk in a procession down to the harbour and along the ancient pier. In fine weather this was a picturesque sight. Despite my denial to the landlady I sometimes joined the students at the Chapel – not entirely out of boredom – because there were occasionally interesting guest preachers who I wanted to hear.

The climate was a minor stumbling block on the road to assimilation. It rained very frequently. I suppose that 'showers and bright intervals' is the most accurate weather forecast for much of the British Isles throughout the year. I just made a habit of never leaving the house without wearing my raincoat, however blue the sky; I knew that sooner or later there would be a heavy downpour. Only a British poet could have written the line 'The rain – it raineth every day'. However, I soon got used to the North Sea climate and indeed, enjoyed its bracing effect. Moreover, I fell in love with the majestic beauty of the Scottish Highlands to which Dan Rutherford introduced me by inviting me to join him and some friends in most delightful walking and climbing expeditions.

At the end of a summer term all St. Andrews students had to vacate their lodgings, because the landladies could let the accommodation more profitably to the visitors who flocked to St. Andrews for the golf season. I was therefore in a dilemma, as I did not know where to go. It would have been disastrous for me to return to Germany for the vacation, although my parents still lived there until 1938.

Unexpectedly, it was the Glasgow mathematicians who came to my rescue in this predicament. They invited me to move to Glasgow where suitable lodgings were found for me. Although I was not a student at Glasgow University, the Librarian provided me with a writing desk in a quiet corner of the library, where I continued to work on my thesis.

In their kindness my hosts even thought of some recreations and holidays for me. In the 1930s Glasgow had been badly hit by the recession and there was a great deal of unemployment especially among the Clyde ship workers. Some of the men had not had a holiday for many years. So the Glasgow students put up a camp on a small island, known as Inchcalliach, in Loch Lomond, near its Eastern shore. They invited a group of unemployed men to spend a week's holiday there. The camp consisted of several large tents, each housing six men and one student whose task it was to entertain the men. I was put in charge of one of the tents. Initially, there was some difficulty in communication: their strong Glaswegian accent did not blend with my foreign intonation, but we soon got on well with one another and engaged in friendly chats. The men were grateful for the hospitality and the opportunity of a holiday. However, I noticed signs of unrest and frustration; the landowner who controlled the Eastern shore of Loch Lomond had refused to grant licences for alcoholic drinks in the region and there was no chance of having a pint of beer in the vicinity. The nearest place where these invigorating beverages could be obtained was at Luss, a village on the West shore of Loch Lomond, at some distance from our camp. I borrowed a large rowing boat from a group of boy scouts who were camping near us on the same little island. Then I selected three of the most needy and thirsty men from my tent who could handle oars, and we rowed across the lake. I had hardly finished fastening the boat at the pier in Luss, when the men made a dash for the nearest pub and disappeared. They were not seen again until it was time to start on our return journey. When they finally came out of the pub it was plain that they were in no condition to hold an oar, let alone share in the rowing. Instead they slumped on to the floor of the boat and remained there motionless. So I had no option but to row the heavily laden craft single-handedly back to our camp. Needless to say I made no further excursions to Luss.

While I was grappling with the Glaswegian accent of my companions, I worked assiduously at improving my knowledge of standard English. It was my intention to obtain the Certificate of Proficiency in English awarded under the auspices of the University of Cambridge. I must have used my leisure on the camp to good effect, because I passed the examination 'with merit' later during the summer.

On my return to St. Andrews I felt increasingly at home in this captivating little town. To some extent St. Andrews had preserved the authority and dignity of the ecclesiastical centre that it possessed in mediaeval times. The magnificent cathedral was destroyed during the Reformation. But the ruins of its walls and those of the castle and other monuments afford an awe-inspiring reminder of its glory, as numerous impressive ancient buildings which are still being used.

Even in 1934, when I arrived the ecclesiastical character of St. Andrews was reflected in the composition of the teaching staff of the University: there were six Full Professors in the Faculty of Divinity, but only one Professor of Mathematics and none of French or German.

The character of the town was maintained by the absence of heavy motor traffic: there were no traffic lights in the town. The nearest point on the main railway line was a place called Leuchars, a few miles distant from St. Andrews to which it was linked by a branch line. The railway station at St. Andrews was closed each Saturday evening and not opened again until Monday morning. Some years ago this rail link was abandoned for economic reasons and replaced by a bus service.

D'Arcy Thompson

The academic community at St. Andrews was small, but very friendly and sociable. Although I was but an insignificant post-graduate student I soon got to know most members of the teaching staff, including the Heads of other Departments. With one of these my encounter had a mathematical aspect. **Sir d'Arcy Thompson** was the Professor of Zoology. He was a man of impressive appearance: a white beard, a strong voice and the bearing of a 'real' professor. He was admired for the remarkable breadth and variety of his knowledge. He had a sonorous voice and was a fluent and powerful speaker. Trained at Trinity College Cambridge, he remained attached to his *alma mater* throughout his life. Even as an old man he would made the journey from St. Andrews to Cambridge in order to take part in a 'Feast'. On one of these occasions I asked him after his return to St. Andrews if he had liked the excursion. He replied: "The company was delightful, but the meal was abysmal. When I was at Trinity, the College could boast of some of the finest kitchens in England. But now they buy their provisions at the Co-Operative Stores. I would willingly spit upon their graves".

Apart from his own subject of biology, he was a highly competent classical scholar and he was fond of exercising his skills as an amateur of mathematics. His masterpiece *Growth and Form* was a classic; in it he used quite sophisticated mathematical methods to elucidate the shapes that occur in the living world and bearing witness to his linguistic prowess the book is replete with long quotations in French, German, Latin and classical Greek (with no English translation). When I met him, he was engaged in writing a new and revised version of his book. One of the topics in which he was interested required the use of differential equations, a subject which evidently lay outside d'Arcy Thompson's field of knowledge at that time. So one day when he saw me in the University Library he said: "Do you know anything about differential equations?" When I replied that I was familiar with this subject, he put his arm on my shoulders and said: "Here is a good boy. Come along with me to my house and tell me all about it." So I went to his house with him, sat down at his desk and wrote out the answer to his question.

When I moved from Berlin to St. Andrews, the strangeness of language, society and climate was to be expected. But I was surprised and, initially embarrassed to find that the attitude to mathematics and the topics taught at St. Andrews were markedly different from the experiences I had as a student in Berlin. For example, I had learned the precise conditions under which a certain type of differential equation would have a unique solution; but when I was confronted with the problem of finding the solution of a particular equation, I needed some time to carry out the task. As was the custom at many British universities, research students at St. Andrews were asked to help with exercise classes given to undergraduates. In the 1930s there were few duplicating machines available. So, the professor or lecturer who took the exercise class wrote a number of problems on the black board at the beginning of the hour. Then, together with his assistants he would walk through the classroom and help the students to write out the solutions. At St. Andrews, the ability to solve unseen problems rapidly was the principal aim of the undergraduate's mathematical education.

Indeed, the final assessment for the award of a degree consists almost entirely of such problems about the various branches of mathematics that had been taught; some questions contained a small amount of 'book work', that is the request to recall certain definitions or standard results; but as a rule only a small number of marks could be gained for book work. Exceptionally, in the examination paper for second year students, there were questions about the history of mathematics, because Turnbull always gave a course of lectures on this subject to young students. The questions in the examination paper were quite impressive; for example: "Give an account either of the Pythagoreans and their work or that of the Alexandrian School". In fact, Turnbull had a keen interest in the history of mathematics. He was the author of the charming little book *The Great Mathematicians* and he had made some major contributions to the history of mathematics, notably through his work on the life of James Gregory and the correspondence of Isaac Newton.

Since the examination paper had to be written in a limited time, normally three hours, speed was of the essence and a good memory was essential, because no access to notes or reference books was allowed. To be sure, as an undergraduate in Berlin I also attended exercise classes, at which problems were written on the blackboard. But the solutions were not to be attempted during the hour; they were left to us to do in our time at home. The notebooks containing our work were handed in and returned the following week with corrections and comments. I have never, to this day, been locked up in a room and expected to solve a number of unseen problems within a specified time.

In the meantime I submitted my doctoral dissertation. It was accepted and, to my relief, it was decided to dispense with an oral examination. In the summer of 1936, little more than two years after my arrival, I was awarded the degree at the colourful ceremony which, I was told, was an ancient tradition at St. Andrews. However, my pleasure of having received the title of a Doctor of Philosophy was soon overshadowed by dread of an uncertain future.

Much had changed since my life in Berlin and the political situation steadily worsened in Germany. I kept in touch with my old friend Walter Jakob even after my emigration to St Andrews. The last letter from Jakob was dated March 1936. He congratulated me on receiving my PhD and mentioned that he too had passed the oral examination for a Doctorate, but had difficulties in finding the money to have his thesis printed, which is a requirement in Germany. When Hitler started the war, Jakob served in the German army, as his father had done twenty-five years before. After the war my friend Alfons Leitl made some enquiries and was told that Walter Jakob had gone 'missing' in Russia.

It was made clear to me that there was no prospect of employment for me at St. Andrews. So Professor Turnbull suggested that I might have a better chance at Edinburgh and he suggested that I should seek an interview with Professor **Edmund Whittaker**, and this was the beginning of the next chapter in my professional life.

V
Edinburgh, 1936 – 8 and Thereafter

During the first half of the last century Professor E.T. Whittaker (Sir Edmund Whittaker, as he was later to be) was one of the most respected and influential mathematicians in the United Kingdom. Indeed, it was said that no Chair of Mathematics anywhere in the British Empire could be filled unless Whittaker's opinion had first been sought. It was therefore with some trepidation that I went to Edinburgh and approached the interview with this powerful person.

E.T. Whittaker

However, within a few minutes Whittaker put me at my ease. He stressed the view, relevant also today, that in times of economic hardship, students should acquire knowledge and experience in many different parts of their subject so as to facilitate employment. He invited me to come to Edinburgh for one term as a visiting student and he offered me a bursary of £50, which I accepted most gratefully. He then continued "I have on my staff **Alec Aitken**, who is an expert on algebra, numerical analysis and statistics. I advise you to attend his lectures and to become familiar with Dr. Aitken's work." After a few seconds he added in a subdued voice: "Don't you see how pale he looks?"

I was taken aback and puzzled by this remark. Did Whittaker expect me to become Aitken's successor? At the time of the interview I was 25 and Aitken was 41 years of age. I had met Aitken on many occasions when I was a research student at St. Andrews, and I always found him lively and energetic. The context of Whittaker's lugubrious observation did not become clear to me until much later.

With Aitken's permission I attended his courses, and I learned a great deal from them. For me Aitken was more than an inspiring teacher: he was a caring and sympathetic friend to whom I owe an immeasurable debt of gratitude. Realizing that my modest bursary could not sustain me for more than a few months, he endeavoured to find a source of income for me. He had the felicitous idea of introducing me to Professor (later Sir) **Godfrey Thomson**, the Professor of Education at Edinburgh. Professor Thomson was interested in using a suitable battery of tests in order to measure a person's intelligence (appropriately defined). The theoretical tools for this investigation required a good deal of mathematics, notably matrix theory, which was closely related to my doctoral dissertation.

I vividly remember my first interview with Godfrey Thomson in the summer of 1936. After introducing me Aitken left the room, and I was about to have two startling experiences. First, Godfrey Thomson addressed me in German. He spoke the language so well that he might have been taken for a native of the country from which I had fled only recently to escape murderous persecution. He told me that before the First World War he had been a student of physics at Strasbourg, which was then a German city. The second surprise came when (now reverting to English) he offered me the position of mathematical assistant for this research project. I accepted his invitation with alacrity and gratitude. It was to be my first opportunity to have a regular income as a mathematician. To be sure, prior permission had to be obtained from the Home Office to remove the ban on my employment; fortunately this was readily accomplished as the money for Thomson's project came from America, and I was not competing with a British candidate.

My work with Godfrey Thomson was inspiring, creative and intimate. We met daily during the morning break at Moray House, where the Department of Education was situated. After we had briefly surveyed the progress of our research on the previous day, Miss **Matthew**, his charming and highly efficient secretary, brought in the coffee and some delicious buttered ginger bread. We then discussed the next stage of our work and returned to our rooms.

The very intensity with which he pursued his ideas, was a great stimulus for me to solve the mathematical problems he had passed on to me. Godfrey Thomson did not claim to be a mathematician. Although he understood mathematical formulae when they were presented to him, he preferred to verify his ideas by constructing elaborate numerical examples from which the theoretical result could be guessed with some confidence. It was then my task to give mathematical proofs of his conjectures, which invariably turned out to be correct.

In 1937 Godfrey Thomson took a year's leave of absence from the university in order to write his book *The Factorial Analysis of Human Ability* (University of London Press, 1939), in which he gave a brilliant account of his ideas on the statistical method known as factor analysis. It was said that during that year no one was allowed to see him except the members of his family, his devoted secretary and myself. For part of the year, especially in the summer, he and his wife stayed at their cottage in Ayrshire. But it was evident that Godfrey Thomson did not go there in order to indulge in a holiday; on the contrary, he immersed himself even more fully in his research work and explored new ideas which he communicated to me by post. I had over one hundred letters from him, beautifully written, often in pencil so that he could make a copy produced with the help of a piece of carbon paper. I treasured these documents, not only on account of their scientific value; they also brought out Godfrey Thomson's warm-hearted personality. In his letters he would often refer to my personal anxieties in those harrowing years before the outbreak of the war. My parents were still in Germany eager to join me in Britain, and my sisters were in Palestine, which was torn by violence and strife. In 2005 I donated my collection of Thomson's letters to the University of Edinburgh, where they are now being used for research purposes.

In 1937 my work with Godfrey Thomson was interrupted for six months when I accepted an unexpected invitation to fill a temporary vacancy in the mathematics department at Dundee, which was then a part of the University of St. Andrews. This was my first teaching experience, and I found it extremely hard. My duties included preparing nine lectures each week covering three different subjects in pure and applied mathematics. I found it convenient to prepare my lectures in my office at the College and would sit there until well after midnight writing my notes.

On one occasion I was nearly arrested by the night watchman who thought I was an intruder with evil intentions. I liked Dundee; it was a friendly place, with a pleasant social life among the faculty members. One Saturday evening, when I turned up at the Staff

Club, I was told that the programme was a 'Clan Whist Drive'. I was at first rather put off by this because I had to confess that I had never played whist and that, with regret, I could not claim adherence to any Scottish Clan. But the organizer of the entertainment reassured me on both points. "We have only three Fergusons here tonight", she informed me, "I am sure they will be pleased to adopt you for this evening so as to complete the team of four players and also teach you how to play whist". The three Fergusons received me with great kindness and evidently found in me an able pupil, for by the end of the evening I had won ten shillings for the Ferguson team which I divided equally between the real and fictitious Fergusons.

After completing the two terms of teaching at Dundee I returned to Edinburgh and continued my collaboration with Godfrey Thomson (as his 'tame mathematician' in Einstein's terminology). I stayed with him for a further twelve months until the autumn of 1938 when I left Edinburgh in order to take up a position at St. Andrews. But I made frequent visits to Edinburgh during the next eight years and, whenever possible, called on him and his wife at their beautiful home. Also, we kept up a lively correspondence especially at the time when he was preparing a second edition of his book and asked for my advice. His last letter to me is dated May 1954, when he congratulated me on the birth of our son but also wanted to know my opinion about a complicated statistical problem that had been raised by another author.

Intensive though my work with Godfrey Thomson was, it did not prevent me from taking part in other stimulating activities. I regularly attended Professor Whittaker's mathematical seminar. The talks given there were of a high standard. Sometimes Professor Whittaker himself would give a series of lectures on topics which in Britain are termed applied mathematics but elsewhere would be called physics. I recall especially a brilliant exposition by Whittaker of a book on elementary particles published by A. Eddington only a few weeks before.

At Edinburgh, like at most British universities, the distinction between applied mathematics and physics is not clearly marked. I believe that the fusion of the two subjects is due to the unique genius of Isaac Newton who made fundamental contributions to both mathematics and physics. The very title of his *Philosophiae Naturalis Principia Mathematica* was used to give the Physics Department at Edinburgh the charmingly atavistic name of Department of Natural Philosophy.

The Chair of Natural Philosophy had recently become vacant, and it was offered to **Max Born**. He was one of the most distinguished scholars who had to leave Germany on account of Hitler's racial persecution. Born had previously been a full professor at Göttingen and thus had occupied one of the most prestigious positions to which a scientist could aspire. He had indeed a world-wide reputation for his outstanding contributions to various branches of theoretical physics. Already as an undergraduate in Berlin I had reason to be grateful to Born. When registering for the State Examination I asked my supervisor to give me a topic that would appeal to a mathematician and he selected a treatise by Max Born on the properties of crystals. I enjoyed reading this book, and I made it the subject of my dissertation.

Now I had the exciting experience of meeting the admired author in person. Born was very approachable and kind to the younger members of the department. He and Mrs. Born frequently invited me to their house, mostly to take part in playing chamber music. Born was an excellent pianist and we had some delightful musical afternoons together.

Sometimes Max Born went for a walk with me and spoke to me about problems in physics that occupied him. One of these was an unpleasant controversy he had with C.V. Raman, the Indian Nobel Laureate. Raman asserted that Born's theory of crystals was unsound, and an acrimonious correspondence ensued which was published in the journal *Nature*. The arguments put forward were couched in rather general and vague terms. I was able to translate them into rigorous mathematical language and to prove that Born's theory was correct and that Raman's objections were invalid.

Max Born

Born was very pleased with my intervention and invited me to join his team of research workers and become a physicist. Although I felt greatly honoured by this offer, I declined it because I felt that I could not, on my own, produce original work as a physicist. I have been very conscious of the difference between mathematics and physics, ever since the physics students in Berlin taunted the mathematicians by saying that their work was 'merely formal'. Of course the results of physics are usually expressed in mathematical terms often involving quite advanced mathematical notions. Nevertheless, to the physicist mathematics is but a language, the content being physics, and the aim is to understand the laws of the universe.

The following incident may serve as an illustration: Whittaker had given a seminar on some aspects of Eddington's 'Fundamental Theory' about the constants occurring in nature. In this particular lecture Whittaker had given a brilliant account of the theory of two particles, the proton and the electron for which Eddington obtained a quadratic equation, whose roots (surprisingly!) are in the ratio of the masses of the two particles. As we were leaving the room after the lecture, Born said to me: "If Eddingtom had considered a

64

system of three particles, I am sure he would have ended up with a cubic equation whose roots are proportional to the masses of the three particles", meaning that in this theory the mathematical formulation took precedent over the physical content.

Born was not offended by my decision not to become a physicist. On the contrary he continued to support me in my career as a mathematician. Shortly after his arrival in Edinburgh Born collected a lively and able group of research students around him. They came from all corners of the world. But as he wistfully reported in his autobiography *My Life*, p.284 (London 1978) only two came from Scotland. The reason, as he rightly points out, was the fact that a talented British student would endeavour to obtain a scholarship for Oxford or Cambridge, which would provide better prospects for his career. He questioned whether this monopoly of Oxford and Cambridge was beneficial to British science.

One of Born's research students was **Klaus Fuchs** who, ten years later, gained shameful notoriety as a traitor and spy. I got to know Fuchs quite well. He was a quiet man who lived modestly in some miserable basement lodgings. I knew that he was not Jewish and I assumed that he left Nazi Germany for political reasons. But he never talked about that or anything else for that matter. I do not believe that Fuchs was a wicked person or that he committed treason for personal gain. The most likely explanation of his action seems to me his fear that the United States, which was then the sole owner of atomic weapons, would launch a pre-emptive atomic war against the Soviet Union. Fuchs argued, correctly as it turned out, that if the Russians also had the atomic bomb neither side would dare to start an atomic war and an unimaginable human catastrophe would be prevented.

Fuchs and I belonged to the same string quartet, in which he played the viola rather indifferently and I played the first violin. We enjoyed playing together. I remember our last musical evening. Towards the end of the summer term in 1938 it became clear that our quartet would probably never meet again, as each of us had accepted appointments in different parts of the country. We decided to meet on a Saturday evening at the spacious lodgings of the second violin in order to enjoy a long session performing all the six quartets that make up Beethoven's opus 18. It was a warm summer's evening and, I fear, our host had left one of the windows slightly ajar to increase ventilation. We had only just begun number 4 of opus 18 when there was a heavy bang at the front door. Our host opened the door and found a large policeman standing outside who said with a stern voice: "Is this the flat where all the noise comes from? (a less than flattering description of Beethoven's string quartet). It can be heard all over the district. Don't you know it is the Sabbath morning (apparently, it was past midnight). You must stop at once." So our music session ended abruptly by order of the police. As we had expected we never met again.

Max Born was in his fifties when he had to leave Germany and he retained some of the continental attitudes and tastes which younger refugees would have discarded. He loved Scotland, but felt a strong affinity to continental Europe. During a recent vacation Born had visited Denmark as a passenger in a small Danish cargo boat that sailed direct from Leith (Edinburgh harbour) to Copenhagen. On his return he related his experiences during a coffee break in his Department: "I am normally a good sailor", he said "but when I saw all the continental sausages and other delicacies on the Danish boat, I nearly became sick through over-indulgence". Whittaker was present at this conversation and commented: "This is an excellent story, Born; I must remember it for your obituary notice".

This somewhat indelicate remark was all the more surprising because Whittaker was nine years Born's senior and in fact died long before him. But the incident was an example of Whittaker's preoccupation with the deaths of his colleagues. Every time an eminent mathematician had died, Whittaker used the opportunity of a meeting of the Edinburgh Mathematical Society to deliver a beautifully balanced eulogy of the deceased mathematician, and I began to wonder whether these speeches were not entirely improvised but were enriched by anecdotes he had collected over the years. I also recalled his unexpected remark about Aitken's health at our first encounter.

One of the most remarkable members of the Mathematics Department at Edinburgh in the 1930s was **William Edge**. He was trained at Cambridge and was most strongly influenced by the renowned geometers who were active at Cambridge in the 1920s. Throughout his life Edge produced a steady stream of substantial memoirs of high quality ,mostly dealing with problems in classical algebraic geometry, and sometimes referring to the application of group theory. He did not seem to be particularly interested in other branches of mathematics. Edge was deeply attached to Cambridge and was proud to have been an alumnus there. In conversation he frequently said: "When I was at Cambridge......" I remember sharing a modest lunch with him in the Refectory during the war, when the only item on the menu was 'sausages and chips'. After a few bites Edge declared with some disgust: "When I was at Cambridge, we had much better sausages." .

He was a life-long bachelor, a tall good looking man, much admired, albeit unilaterally by some of the young ladies in his class room. He was a good lecturer, speaking with a firm melodious voice which had retained a strong native Lancastrian accent. I recall a dinner party at the Whittaker's where several guests, including myself, had come from abroad and spoke with a foreign accent. The guest of honour was an eminent academic whose wife, an upper class English lady, asked each foreign born guest what their country of origin was. Then she turned to Edge and, embarrassingly, asked: "Where you do come from?" In his personal relations Edge was aloof and reserved. I have never heard him use a first name when addressing a person, and all his colleagues called him "Edge" at work, and began a letter to him with "Dear Edge....."

He expected a high standard from his students. It seems that during the three decades when he was an active faculty member he had only one research student. Almost throughout his life Edge enjoyed good health. It was his custom every day after lunch to travel by bus to the outskirts of Edinburgh and after a long and strenuous country walk, to return to the Mathematics Department in the late afternoon. However, some time during the war, Whittaker had to tell us that black-out regulations made it necessary to revise the timetable and that henceforth some lectures would have to given at two o'clock instead of later in the day. Edge realized that this would deprive him of his favourite country walk at least on some days of the week. He expressed his indignation with the words: "Sir, a gentleman does not work in the afternoon."

William Edge

Edge was a staunch Roman Catholic. I had the impression that he did not like foreigners, even less when they were Jewish. There were reports that he made derogatory remarks about them. Nevertheless, a person who was relatively close to him was **Robin Schlapp**, Reader in Applied Mathematics. Robin's parents had come from Germany and his father was Professor of German Literature at Edinburgh University. But Robin was born in Scotland and studied at Cambridge. He was not Jewish and I suppose this fully legitimized him in the eyes of Edge.

Although Edge was a man of few words in conversation he could express himself well in music He was a very good pianist and was willing to join companions in the joy of chamber music. Robin Schlapp was an excellent cellist and he too was lover of chamber music – more about this later.

The very antithesis to Edge amongst the faculty members was **Ivor Etherington** (he had been a student at Oxford!). He and his wife frequently offered generous hospitality to colleagues and friends, and especially to the victims of Hitler's persecution. Ivor was always ready to help in every possible way; it was typical of him that he got up from his seat about 10 minutes before the end of the seminar and put the iron kettle on the open fire so that tea could be made for every one as soon as the seminar was over. Later he took on a heavy burden of administrative duties. Etherington had a wide knowledge of mathematics. One could go for a walk with him and talk about one's research problem and be sure that Ivor would listen with understanding and offer useful advice and suggestions. During the 1930's Etherington had adopted some left-wing political ideas and he made no secret of his sympathies. Occasionally there were animated, but always good-natured discussions over tea after the seminar, when Ivor's views clashed with Whittaker's more conventional and religious convictions. Whittaker was a convert to Catholicism and was strict in his observance.

I played chamber music with friends inside and outside the university. In particular, I was a member of what I might call the Mathematical Piano Quartet. It consisted of Edge (piano), Aitken (violin), myself (viola) and Schlapp (cello). We had not much time to practice together and reached only a modest standard of proficiency. In fact we never got further than playing the two lovely piano quartets by Mozart in G-minor and E-flat major respectively. Nevertheless, our quartet played a distinctive social role in the Mathematics Department. The meeting of the Edinburgh Mathematics Seminar was usually on the first Friday of each month during the academic term. After the meeting Professor and Mrs Whittaker always gave a dinner party at their beautiful house, to which the speaker at the Seminar and other guests were invited. Whittaker did not like trivial conversation. Therefore he always invited guests who would entertain the company with some musical offering, and this invariably included our quartet.

The dinner was very formal, such as might be described in a Victorian novel. First soup was served and then fish. This was followed by meat, usually roast beef but since the dinner took place on a Friday, Whittaker and Edge, being strict Catholics, refrained from eating meat and were served a second helping of fish. After the dessert had been eaten, the ladies left the dining room and went upstairs, the men staying behind. When a suitable time had elapsed, Whittaker said: "Gentlemen, shall we join the ladies?" Then all the guests settled down in the drawing room around the piano and Whittaker asked for musical contributions.

When Turnbull was among the guests he began the playing; he was a good pianist, and did not seem to mind playing before an audience. Sometimes other solo pieces were played on the piano. But the main item in the programme was undoubtedly our piano quartet. On alternate months we played one or the other of the Mozart quartets, since alas these were our total repertory. This continued for several years. But Whittaker always applauded us with the words: "This was delightful; have I heard it before?"

During one month there was a minor crisis: an extra meeting of the Edinburgh Mathematical Society was to take place, at which a distinguished visitor was going to give a lecture. As usual, there was going to be a dinner party at the Whittaker's, to which the quartet was invited. But Aitken said: "We can't play the Mozart quartet again; we have just done it. Let us try something else!" We met at Edge's lodgings for a rehearsal and played a little of one of the Brahms quartets. However, it soon became clear it was too difficult and that we should be unable to master in the short time at our disposal. So with his whimsical humour Aitken suggested: "Let us play a simple Haydn trio for piano, violin and cello and Walter will look at a music stand in front of him and pretend to play his viola, so that it looks as if we were performing a quartet." We rehearsed the sham quartet for a while; but we soon gave it up since we could not hide our mirth and moreover realized that our deception would surely be discovered in the confined space of the Whittaker's drawing room. So we decided, of necessity, to play one the Mozart quartets after all. The performance went well and was warmly praised by Whittaker with the words: "This was delightful. Have I heard it before?"

My experiences at Edinburgh are very precious to me. It is a beautiful city; in the years when I lived there even more so than today, after some of the picturesque establishments have been replaced by chain stores and mass-produced eating places. There was a flourishing cultural life and an attractive neighbourhood which offered refreshing walks and excursions. Although I was not a registered student or member of faculty at the University, I have formed a lasting bond with the academic institutions that are associated with Edinburgh. In 1940 I was awarded the degree of Doctor of Science for my contributions to Godfrey Thomson's research programme which he had published in *The Factorial Analysis of Human Abilities*, a book that rapidly went to several editions. In 1944, I was elected a Fellow of the Royal Society of Edinburgh; I regret that I am now unable to attend its meetings; but I am always pleased to be informed about its activities and to be reminded of my life in Edinburgh.

VI
Start of my Academic Career

Every four years, except for a rather long interruption caused by the war, the Edinburgh Mathematical Society organized a Mathematical Colloquium to be held for several days in the summer. The venue was St. Andrews, where it was attractive to stay in the summer; in addition, since the students had gone home, the spacious residential homes offered the participants comfortable accommodation. Members of their families were welcome to join them and provisions were made to those who did not wish to take part in the mathematical activities. The standard of the mathematical presentations was high. Usually some eminent British or foreign mathematicians were invited to give one or more lectures as part of the varied and stimulating programme. But the organizers did not neglect the social aspect of the conference. There were plenty of opportunities to meet other participants and their families. In the evenings there were enjoyable performances of chamber music by members of the conference and the quality of string quartet playing rivaled that of the mathematical lectures offered earlier that day. On one occasion a complete Bach Cantata was performed in which Edge sang the solo part and Schlapp played the double bass instead of the cello, which was his usual instrument.

One such colloquium took place in July 1938. Dan Rutherford acted as the local secretary. He asked me to be an assistant secretary, which I was very willing to be. The invitation to the foreign visitors and most of the programme had already been arranged by the senior members of the organizing committee. I was mainly concerned with the social and domestic aspects of the conference. But the experience was valuable to me.

Shortly before the Colloquium started, Professor Turnbull unexpectedly asked me to see him. He told me that a member of his staff had decided to leave at rather short notice and he invited me to fill the vacancy. Of course, I was delighted to receive this offer; but then he added: "I have to tell you that the post is for applied mathematics; so most of your teaching will be in applied mathematics" My heart sank and I replied meekly: " But I do not know any applied mathematics". With the greatest regret I thought I ought to decline this highly tempting offer. However, Turnbull consoled me: "That does not matter, Walter. We are now at the beginning of July and term does not start until October. So you have plenty of time to prepare your lectures on applied mathematics." With his encouragement I accepted the offer most gratefully. A few days later Professor Turnbull confirmed the appointment in a hand-written letter covering two full pages. I should like to quote some passages from this letter, as it was characteristic of Turnbull's kindness and caring attitude towards young members of the profession.

The University
St Andrews
16.7.38
W. Ledermann Esq. Ph.D.

My dear Walter,
Following our talk the other day I have much pleasure in formally offering you the post of Assistant in the Mathematics Department here for the coming year from October 1938 at the salary of £325. The post is for one year in the first instance, & is capable of renewal. It will involve from 8 to 10 lectures or tutorials a week in mathematics pure and applied......

I naturally look back on my start at lecturing in thinking of your present position. My first post outside Cambridge (where I gave one course a term) was at Liverpool & involved at least 3 sets of new lectures to be prepared, & in one term 4 sets.......

I hope you will have a good holiday in Wales with your brother. Please give him my kind regards. Llanfairfechen on the coast is a good centre for combining sea & hill walking.......

With best wishes
Yours very sincerely.
H.W. Turnbull

73

It was courageous of Turnbull to offer me the appointment. In 1938 I was still a foreigner –and a 'German' to boot. My situation as a refugee was not generally understood. I remember that, shortly after I obtained the Ph.D. degree, the Professor of Philosophy, who was a kindly gentlemen, said to me: "You were welcome to take the doctorate here; but now we expect you to go home." I was told later that, when the Senate of the University met again after the summer vacation, Turnbull was severely criticized by some of his colleagues who insisted that "we want our own people." There was even a rumour that at one point Turnbull indicated that he would resign from the Regius Chair of Mathematics at St. Andrews. Fortunately, no action was taken, although I sensed a coolness towards me on the part of some senior members of the University. However, my appointment was renewed each year until 1945 when it was made permanent.

During the next two months I immersed myself in the large textbook literature on Mechanics in order to prepare the required lectures and tutorials in applied mathematics. I was familiar with the general principles of mechanics, which I had learned from lectures by R. von Mises in Berlin. But I had no experience of solving complicated problems involving various objects sliding down an inclined plane or elastic spheres being in collision. By looking at examination papers of previous years I realized that this was precisely what I had to teach my students. It became clear to me that there was a fundamental difference in the training of students of mathematics in Britain and on the Continent. To put it succinctly, perhaps with some bias and exaggeration, I am tempted to say that German students are taught to talk about mathematics; but British students are trained to do mathematics.

I hope I discharged my duties as a teacher of applied mathematics in a satisfactory manner. I liked my students and enjoyed the friendly atmosphere in the mathematics department. But I have reservations concerning the subject; for to my mind, mechanics, which is what applied mathematics is really about, forms a very important part of physics, a study of the laws that govern the motion of material objects. To be sure, these laws are expressed in the language of mathematics. But we must guard against confounding form and content. Mathematics is used in many other disciplines. The modeling of market risks requires quite sophisticated mathematics; yet, our students are not taught the principles of financial management. It is true that there have been individuals, the outstanding example being Isaac Newton, who were masters of both mathematics and physics. But this does not justify the demand that every mathematician must be proficient in physics or even in parts of it. My view is that while physics has a great deal to do with mathematics, mathematics has nothing to do with physics.

Although the bulk of my teaching was in applied mathematics, as I was told at the time of my appointment, I was pleased that occasionally Professor Turnbull allowed me to give a course on pure mathematics, which I enjoyed very much more. In 1938 the Department consisted of five people: Turnbull, the only Professor; **E.T. Copson**, who later succeeded Turnbull in the Chair; Dan Rutherford and **Geoffrey Timms** as Lectures or Senior Lecturers; and myself. Timms was a quiet and very reserved man. He was a geometer of the classical school. Dan was the senior member responsible for applied mathematics, although his doctoral dissertation, like mine, was on an algebraic topic. I once heard a colleague in another university ridicule St. Andrews as the place were applied mathematics is represented by two algebraists. The teaching load for the five faculty members was heavy, because the degree course at a Scottish university extended over four years. The four stages are referred to as General Class, Special Class, Junior Honours Class and Senior Honours Class, each having separate lectures, exercise classes and examination papers.

With so much effort expended on teaching and examining it is not surprising that research did not flourish as much as one might have hoped. There were only a few post-graduate students and we had no regular research seminars. Occasionally members of the faculty reported on their research: Timms and Turnbull speaking about topics in geometry. Regrettably, I derived no stimulation for original work from my colleagues at St. Andrews. Perhaps I was occupied too much with my teaching duties. A little more than a year after my appointment war broke out and I was engaged in some war work (to be described in the next chapter), which I carried out in addition to my university duties. I enjoyed lecturing and was always pleased to meet my students, to get to know them individually and to help during the exercise classes.

My mind went back to the time when I was a student in Berlin. I remembered how much I benefited from reading the pocket-sized (10cm by 15cm) books of the *Göschen Sammlung*, each of about 180 pages bound in dark-yellow cloth. They included some excellent volumes, for instance, two by Helmut Hasse on Algebra and two by Konrad Knopp on Complex Analysis. I always carried one of these booklets in my pocket and read it during the dreary railway journey from my parents' home to the University. It occurred to me that there did not seem to be a similar set of mathematics textbooks in English (the Methuen Monographs were mostly about Physics). I passed on my observation to my friend Dan Rutherford. He was interested in the idea and discussed it with the Edinburgh publishers Oliver & Boyd and it was agreed to launch the blue series *University Mathematical Texts*. After informing me of the successful outcome of his negotiations, Dan added: "Although it was your idea, Walter, you will understand that we will not put your name on these books. People will not like to see a German name on them. I have therefore asked Alec Aitken to be one of the editors. However, after the war I was asked to contribute a book on Group Theory to the series.

My time at St Andrews, 1938 – 46, included the whole period of the Second World War and was therefore dominated by the terrible events that happened to this country and elsewhere. Initially, at a personal level, my anxiety was increased by the fear for the safety of my parents who were still living in Berlin until December 1938 when they were able to join my brother and me in Britain.

Despite the deep shadow that the war cast over all of us, I also had happy experiences and, was generally content with my life at St. Andrews. Quite frequently, Dan invited me and other friends to go on excursions to the Scottish Highlands. We stayed at Youth Hostels and mingled with young people. I was greatly impressed by the beautiful scenery, and I enjoyed exhilarating hill walks. Later on

Dan rented a cottage in Glen Lyon, in a remote part of Perthshire. It was a cosy little house with accommodation for four people.

Only on rare occasions did **Norah Rutherford** (Dan's wife) stay at the cottage. Usually, Dan invited two or three friends to make up an all male mathematical party. The main room, which served as kitchen and dining room, was fitted with a 'black board' consisting of a large piece of dark linoleum nailed to the wall. After dinner we sometimes had a mathematical session, in which we discussed special problems or read together a textbook on a less familiar topic. But for the main part, a stay at the cottage was intended as a holiday with walks and other activities. Although food was rationed during the war, we had enough to eat. Nevertheless, some supplements were welcome. Dan was a skilful angler. He had permission to fish in the nearby river and often brought back some sizeable trout, which made a delicious dinner. One day, unwisely, I asked for the loan of a fishing rod and went down to the river to try my luck at the sport. But my attempt at casting was so clumsy that the line rebounded and the barbed hook got embedded in my finger. Dan had to call on the gamekeeper in the neighbouring estate, who came to the cottage and freed my hand from the painful injury.

One morning, all of us who were staying at the cottage went for a stroll in a nearby wood. I noticed a large cluster of yellow mushrooms under a tree. I am not an expert on mushrooms; but I knew that this particular kind, called chanterelle, was edible and in fact very tasty. It is quite popular on the Continent, though rarely seen in British shops, as it is widely believed that all mushrooms, except the white meadow mushroom, are poisonous. As we were filling a hat with the yellow chanterelles, the farmer observed us from the other side of the river and shouted across: "What are you doing?" Dan answered: "We are picking mushrooms for our dinner". The farmer asked: "How many are you at the cottage?" Dan said: "Four." And we received the decisive answer: "I shall send four coffins to the cottage tomorrow." When we got back to the cottage with our harvest, Dan was a little skeptical. Perhaps he thought the farmer had a point after all. So he said: "Let us fry the mushrooms. Walter will have some for his tea. If he is still alive, we shall all eat the rest for our supper."

There was a flourishing musical life at St. Andrews with numerous participants from both the 'town' and the 'gown' sections of the community. Being a small town and outside the main line of communication, St. Andrews was not visited by professional orchestras or operatic companies. So, music lovers were all the more encouraged to make their own music. There was an annual amateur performance of the *Messiah*, in which I played the viola. I met several good pianists with whom I played violin sonatas. But my greatest pleasure was to play chamber music, usually as second violin with a group of competent amateurs. On a few occasions the Music Department of the University arranged visits for celebrated artists. I remember a recital by Myra Hess. It was my duty to provide her with a piano stool; she was not easy to please and rejected my first offer of what I thought was a suitable piece of furniture. A visit from the Griller Quartet was a great joy. It was one of the finest performances of chamber music I have ever heard.

In 1939 the University of St. Andrews decided to establish a department of astronomy. A modern observatory was to be built near the University with facilities for teaching and research. The person who was to be in charge of these developments was **Erwin Freundlich**. At the time of his appointment to the post at St. Andrews, he was already in his mid-fifties and had a world-wide reputation as an astronomer. Freundlich was not Jewish. His father was a German businessman and his mother was British; her maiden name was Finlayson. When he settled in St. Andrews, he added 'Finlay' to his name, which is Scottish, and he was henceforth called Erwin Finlay Freundlich. However his wife was Jewish and when his wife's sister died in 1933, they adopted her children.

It was therefore to be expected that his wife and the children would suffer racial persecution under the Nazis. Freundlich decided to leave Germany and, like a number of other senior German academics who were affected by the racial laws of the Nazis, he accepted a position at the University of Istanbul, where one of his tasks was to supervise the building of a modern observatory. Although he was well paid, he found the conditions uncongenial. It seems that professors were treated in some ways like servants. At the end of the semester he had to fill in a form giving an account of his work. One of the questions was: "How often have you been late for your lecture?"; to which he replied proudly: "I cannot be late for my lecture, because my lecture begins with me." Evidently, a sense of humour was not a strong point with the administrators of the University: he was ordered to appear before the Principal and apologize for insulting the authorities,

Not surprisingly, Freundlich was pleased to accept an invitation from the Charles University of Prague, where he was asked to help with the construction of an observatory. However, his stay was cut short by Hitler's invasion of Czechoslovakia. He fled with his family to Holland, where he received the offer to come to St. Andrews and, for the third time, he was asked to help with the construction of an observatory.

From the beginning, although Freundlich was twenty-six years my senior, I felt close to him. We were the only two persons with a continental background, which brought us naturally together. He was a fatherly friend and I often visited him and his wife in their attractive house on the outskirts of St. Andrews, which was adorned by a striking oil painting of Freundlich by Max Pechstein. On one occasion Freundlich and I went on holiday to the West Coast of Scotland, when his wife was unable to go with him. He was a tall impressive looking man. When we walked from the observatory back to the centre of the city, people would say: "Here comes the Sun and the Moon".

Freundlich was a keen and able cellist. We played piano trios in his house with an excellent young pianist. But our greatest joy was to play string quartets, or sometimes string quintets, in the house of a Scottish clergyman who played the viola. The quartet was led by Mary Lakeman a student at the University. She was an excellent violist, very charming and much admired. Freundlich had a remarkable academic career. After obtaining his doctorate in pure mathematics at the University of Göttingen, he was engaged as an assistant to Einstein at the Observatory near Berlin. Contrary to popular belief, Einstein was not a strong mathematician. His genius lay in having a profound intuitive understanding of the laws of physics that had not previously been thought of, but he required the services of a mathematician ("my tame mathematician", as he called him) in order to express his ideas in rigorous mathematical terms.

Erwin Freundlich

Freundlich told me that one day Einstein came to his office and expounded some of the ideas of his General Relativity theory, on which he was working at that time. Einstein suggested that geometrical relations in space would not follow the Euclidean pattern and that, for example, the shortest distance between two points would not be the straight line joining them but a certain curve. Freundlich said: "Professor Einstein, what you have described is known to mathematicians as Riemannian geometry. It was discovered more than fifty years ago by Bernhard Riemann and developed by him." Einstein was so flabbergasted by this revelation that he blurted out: "Freundlich, you are a liar." But Freundlich made his point by going to the Library and producing a copy of Riemann's original paper. Ever since then, it has been accepted that the General Theory of Relativity is formulated using the terms of Riemannian geometry.

Freundlich's main interest throughout his life was to test the predictions of General Relativity by direct observation. One of the effects predicted by the Theory is the Light Deflection: if light from a star passes near the sun, then its beam will be deflected by 1.75 degrees. Of course, normally a star near the sun cannot be observed during the day, because its light will be obliterated by the much brighter sun. But such an observation would be possible during an eclipse of the sun.

In 1929 Freundlich led a well-equipped and carefully planned expedition to the Indonesian island of Sumatra where a suitable eclipse of the sun was due to occur. However, to his surprise and embarrassment, the observed light deflection was equal to 2.2 degrees and thus substantially larger than the value predicted by the Theory. Unfortunately, several attempts to determine the correct value by repeating the observation elsewhere were frustrated by bad weather.

As far as I know the matter remained undecided during Freundlich's life. The evaluation of the observed data requires a fair amount of mathematical manipulation, which Freundlich explained to me. I was able to offer some technical contributions and these were published in our joint paper *The Problem of an Accurate Determination of the Relativistic Light Deflection* – my only modest foray into the field of astronomy. Whatever the academic merits of this paper, it was of the utmost importance in my personal life, as I shall relate later.

The experiences I had while I lived in St. Andrews from 1938 to 1946 were very precious to me. I am grateful for the friendship and kindness I received, and I enjoyed my work at the University. My attachment to Scotland has remained undiminished all my life.

VII
War Experiences and Marriage

With increasing anxiety and despair I watched Hitler's stunning successes in the 1930s: The Rhineland, Austria, Czechoslovakia ….; there was nothing to stop him. Looking back to those fateful years, one understands how lucky Hitler was. The leaders of the West were generally weak and misguided and failed to understand the true aim of the Nazi dictator. In the face of the rapid and powerful rearmament of the Fascist countries, many people in the western democracies clung to pacifist ideals and disregarded the Roman adage "if you want peace, prepare for war". But the main reason for Hitler's triumphs was the fact that many people in the West believed that Russian Communism was their real enemy and, with some justification, they regarded Hitler as their natural ally in their fight against this evil. It was therefore a shattering blow to any hope for peace when, late in August 1939, Stalin accepted Hitler's offer of a non-aggression pact between Germany and Russia, 'which could not be cancelled within twenty-five years'. (It lasted less than two years.) This was the signal for Hitler to launch the war against Poland, to be followed by the conquests of Denmark and Norway. For Britain, this period was the 'phoney' war, before fighting started in Western Europe.

I was very lucky that just before these events, namely on 11th April 1940, my application for naturalization came through. After the outbreak of hostilities in the West no further applications were considered. The Procurator Fiscal (Justice of the Peace) travelled from the quiet capital of Fife to interview me at St. Andrews. He was a nice elderly gentleman; I doubt whether he had ever seen a foreigner before. He was old enough to remember the First World War and naturally was most concerned about the fact that this country was again at war. "Is it not terrible that we now have another war; so many people will get killed as in the last war", and he added in a subdued voice: "In this war, are you on our side?" I assured him emphatically that I was certainly on his side in this war against Hitler, and I should be glad to do my utmost to help in the war effort. He was satisfied and said: "Sign here and *swear by Almighty God that I will be faithful and bear true allegiance to His Majesty, King George the Sixth, His Heirs and Successors, according to law...*"

I was now a twenty-nine year old male British citizen and was therefore liable to be enlisted in the Armed Forces to serve in the war. First of all I was instructed to report for a medical examination at some place in Dundee. This happened to be on the first Monday of a month and on that day all recruits would be sent to the Navy. I was quite looking forward to being a sailor.

Walter Ledermann

However, at that time of my life I was rather short-sighted and always had to wear spectacles. When I reached the military establishment where the medical examination was to be carried out, the guard at the door stopped me and said: "No sailor ever wears spectacles. Go down to the basement of this building; there is an army Major who will interview our rejects." The Major looked at my papers. "You are a mathematician?" "Yes, Sir." "Can you drive a car?" "I regret: no, Sir." "Then go back to St. Andrews".

However, a few days later I received an Enlistment Notice, telling me to present myself at the Royal Army Pay Corps at Perth. The Notice was accompanied by a nicely produced leaflet with two pictures of the smiling King, in uniform, on the outside and some friendly and helpful and homely pieces of advice on the inside, from Anthony Eden, who was Secretary of State for War. It began by telling you: "*You are about to become a soldier. This will mean a big change in your life.*" And it continued: "*At first, naturally, you will feel rather strange to your surroundings: you will miss your home and friends,...... But.... learn to obey all orders smartly and without question.*" The leaflet ends with the resounding: "*Once more I welcome you to the Army. Fear God, honour the King, and may victory soon crown our arms!*" A postal order for 4 shillings was enclosed 'in respect of advance of service pay'.

I made an appointment with **Sir James Irvine**, the Vice-Chancellor of St. Andrews University, in order to say goodbye before joining the army. When he saw my Enlistment Notice he became angry and said: "Surely, they could make better use of you than putting you as a Private into the Royal Army Pay Corps. Besides, it is a waste of money. The University would have to supplement your army pay so that it is equal to that of a lecturer, because it has been agreed that nobody should lose money by joining the Armed Forces. In addition, we should have to find a replacement for you in the Mathematics Department, because the teaching programme of the University will have to continue. I shall talk to Anthony Eden, who is a friend of mine and tell him that this will not do." As I was leaving his office, he asked his secretary to put a call through to the Secretary State for War. Evidently, Sir James Irvine's intervention was successful, because a few days later I was informed that 'as a result of unforeseen circumstances' my enlistment has been cancelled and I was requested to return the postal order,

I had now been rejected by both the Navy and the Army. But a new opportunity soon presented itself: the University of St. Andrews was chosen to accommodate an Initial Training Wing of the Royal Air Force, where the cadets attended a fairly intensive course of theoretical instruction before they moved on to be trained as pilots. The group was led by a nice and cultured Wing Commander who had been wounded in the battle of Britain a few months earlier and was unable to carry out flying duties. The course included some work on navigation which required a certain amount of mathematical expertise. Dan Rutherford, Freundlich and I were appointed to be part time instructors. Dan received the rank of a Flight Lieutenant, whilst Freundlich and I remained civilians. It did not seem to worry the authorities that two of the three instructors were former foreigners.

I continued with my normal university teaching; now most of the students were women, the men having been called up for military service. My commitment to the Royal Air Force for the remaining four years of the war was quite intensive, with only six days holiday every year. But I enjoyed the work. Since at any time the group of cadets was not large, we were able to get to know the students individually. During the short break in the teaching Dan sometimes arranged excursions to the Highlands. Some of the boys who had come from the South of England had never seen a mountain and found hill climbing the most strenuous part of their training.

There were other ways of contributing very modestly to the war effort. The Royal Army Education Corps engaged lecturers who would go to remote military establishments and talk to the troops on some entertaining and perhaps mildly educational topic. I was invited to be one of the speakers. But I pointed out that, being a mathematician, my own subject would certainly not be entertaining and would be unwelcome. However, I offered to speak on my memories as a child in Berlin. from 1922 to 1923 Germany suffered from 'hyperinflation' which resulted in the almost total destruction of the currency. Bank notes were printed day and night to keep pace with the rapid devaluation. When the nightmare was past and a new currency was introduced, one 'new' mark was equal to one million million 'old' marks. Of course, the old bank notes had no monetary value.

At that time I was twelve years old, and I collected the obsolete money as a toy and to this day I have a box filled with these bizarre mementoes. I passed them round my audience during my lecture on *The German Inflation* and I related some of the sad stories about the hardship suffered by innocent victims of this upheaval. I gave this lecture at several military establishments; but the reception was at best lukewarm. At one artillery unit overlooking the Firth of Forth, the attendance was particularly small: I learned later that the Commandant had designated my lecture a 'defaulters' parade, that is to say, attendance was compulsory for soldiers who had misbehaved in some way. However, one day a more attractive opportunity seemed to arise: I was asked to give my lecture to group of WRNS (Women's Royal Navy Service), and I was looking forward to spending an afternoon with the young ladies. I went to 'His Majesty's Ship', actually a disused school house on the banks of the river Tay in Dundee. The Commandant, a woman in an elegant uniform received me in true naval tradition by handing me a glass of rum. After some polite conversation she said: "Please remind me what your lecture is about." I told her that I would speak about the German inflation. After a few seconds she replied: "Ah, I see. Would you mind if the girls bring their knitting?" Despite this anticlimax I enjoyed the afternoon.

From time to time the Royal Army Education Corps provided Refresher Courses for the teachers in the Education Corps, so that they could consolidate their knowledge and become acquainted with new topics. The Major in charge of the course asked me to contribute with some lectures. I told him that I was very willing to help, but that I did not think mathematics would be a suitable subject. However, in a low voice, as if to divulge some mystery, he said: "I understand that there are two kinds of fractions: vulgar fractions and decimal fractions. Do you think you could explain their difference?" I assured him that I would do my best to satisfy his request.

I went straight to the bookshop and bought a copy of *Brush up your Arithmetic* in order to get some idea about how to treat such an elementary topic. The Major was pleased with my lectures on fractions. He came to see me again and said: "Well done. Could you continue and get as far as LOGARITHMS?" I told him that I did not think this would be feasible and I made no further contributions to the Refresher Course.

I joined the First Aid Team which had to go into action in the event of an air raid alarm. A doctor trained us in rudimentary care, such as the use of the stretcher and how to get wounded persons out of the rubble in a bombed house. Fortunately, we had very few alarms at St. Andrews. But I remember one occasion when in the middle of the night, with no lights, I had to go on my bicycle to the assigned station, which was the female students' Hall of Residence. I spent some pleasant hours there until the All Clear was sounded in the morning.

During the latter part of the war, units of foreign troops were stationed for retraining in some parts of Scotland, including St. Andrews. I spoke to the Minister of the Church of a neighbouring village about this matter and he said: "Oh yes, we had foreign soldiers billeted on us already last year. It was clear that the chaps had more interest in our girls than in their military exercises. Indeed, nine months after their arrival we had a 'lambing season'."

At that time I was warden of a men's Hall of Residence at St. Andrews. One night I was rang up by a man. He had a foreign accent and was very agitated: "Are you Doctor Ledermann? Please come at once. My wife is having a baby." I conveyed to him my best wishes on this happy event; but I told him that I could do nothing about it. He got very angry: "You are a doctor and it is your duty to come and help my wife." He was in no mood to listen to my explanation of academic degrees. His final fling was: "But you have been so warmly recommended!" Fortunately, I was able to give him the name and address of a 'real' doctor, who would surely do what was expected of him.

One curious consequence of the war was my acquaintance with Lady **Elisabeth Babington Smith.** One of my colleagues at St. Andrews was **Bernard Babington Smith.** He was a lecturer in the Department of Experimental Psychology and a specialist in statistics. Occasionally, we talked about mathematical aspects of his work. Some time after the outbreak of the war, he said to me: "I am leaving St. Andrews in order to join the Royal Air Force. Please do me the favour of looking after my mother when she needs company. His mother was the daughter of the 9th Earl of Elgin, who was Viceroy of India in the last decade of the 19th century. One member of his staff was Sir Henry Babington Smith, an eminent civil servant and a renowned expert on international finance. In 1898, at Simla, Sir Henry married Lady Elisabeth Mary Bruce, the family name of Lord Elgin was Bruce, and a descendent of the Scottish King. Evidently it was a happy marriage and they had ten children. Sadly, Sir Henry Babington Smith died in 1923, a few days after the twenty-fifth anniversary of their wedding.

When I first met The Lady Elisabeth she had already been a widow for about twenty years. She lived in a small cottage on the outskirts of St. Andrews and had a very simple life style, as well as a simple way of dressing. One could not guess that she was a member of one of the oldest aristocratic families of Scotland. I do not know whether she had a domestic servant during the week, but Bernard had asked me to visit his mother every Sunday evening, so that she would not be alone then. I enjoyed these occasions very much. She cooked a simple supper for us: two pigeons which she boiled in a casserole. I was fascinated to listen to her stories which she told in a beautiful melodious voice. As a young woman, when her father Lord Elgin was the Viceroy of India, she sometimes had to be the hostess at official functions when her mother was unwell. Her husband was financial advisor to the Turkish government for several years. She was obviously very popular there; she received the Highest Order of the First Class. Our meetings took place in the middle of the war, when our thoughts were with Churchill. I asked her: "Have you met Churchill?" She replied: "Yes, as a young man, he was on father's staff" and she added with a smile: "Mr. Churchill is clever; but he is not wise." In her Will she left me a beautiful bookcase and a ring, that is a ring from a descendant of Robert the Bruce, King of Scotland – should I have laid claim to the Throne of Scotland?

With these diverse activities and duties, the last two years of the war passed quickly, especially since it became increasingly likely that Hitler was going to be defeated (we did not think of an atomic bomb). When, finally, the longed-for Victory in Europe Day came,

88

after Germany's surrender on 8th May 1945, there was enormous relief, although the war in the Far East was not yet over. Freundlich said to me: "Ledermann, now that the war is over, you should get married." I replied: "You may well be right, Professor. But it takes two for such a step." Freundlich was prepared for this query: "I know exactly the young lady who, I hope, will be your wife.

When Freundlich was working in Prague he met **Alice Low-Beer**, whose husband **Walter Low-Beer** was a wealthy business man. Alice and Ruth (**Rushi**) were cousins, their fathers being brothers; but there was a considerable age difference between them. Alice was eighteen years older than Rushi. After the fall of Czechoslovakia the Low-Beers settled in a beautiful house in Epsom, Surrey. Sadly by that time, Walter had suffered a stroke and had become an invalid. Rushi often stayed with her cousin in Epsom. Freundlich also visited the Low-Beers and evidently had met Rushi there and (understandably!) was very impressed by her. Some time during the summer vacation of 1945 he invited Rushi to come to St. Andrews, although he must have known that I was then staying with my parents in London. Our joint paper on the *Relativistic Light Deflection* was then in the process of publication, and both authors were required to read the proof sheets for corrections and return them to the printers. He gave Rushi my London address and asked her to give me a set of proof sheets in person. Thus on one afternoon in the summer of 1945 she appeared at my parents' flat at 10 Church Crescent, Muswell Hill, London N10. She introduced herself and said that Professor Freundlich had asked her to pass on some papers to me.

We soon found that we had much in common. There was a nice piano in my parents' flat and we started playing sonatas for violin and piano straight away. We met several times in London and I visited her at Tunbridge, where she had a position as a social worker at a child guidance clinic. We decided to get married in the spring of the following year, 15th March 1946. Our marriage took place in the morning of that day at the Registry Office in Epsom, since neither of us belonged to a synagogue; but in the afternoon we had a beautiful religious ceremony at the Low-Beer's house. It was conducted by Rabbi Eschelbacher, an old friend of the Stadler family who, I was told, had officiated at the marriage of Rushi's parents in 1913. (Rushi's maiden name is Stadler.)

Ruth (Rushi) Ledermann

We spent the first University term of our married life in furnished rooms at St. Andrews. This was not particularly comfortable. Moreover since St. Andrews is a small town, it had no Child Guidance Clinic, where Rushi could find work. She was offered part-time employment in Dundee, but this was inconvenient as it involved a tedious journey. So, we decided that we would move to more stimulating surroundings, preferably to a city with a flourishing cultural life and a cosmopolitan atmosphere.

VIII
Manchester, 1946 – 62

I had always been attracted to Manchester, a place of intellectual excellence and the home of the famous Hallé Orchestra. During the war, the Mathematics Department at Manchester University was small but it included some renowned scholars. The Head of Department was **Louis Mordell** a distinguished mathematician who, unfortunately, was of a rather selfish disposition. On a war-time visit to Manchester I asked Mordell whether there was any prospect of employment for me and he offered me the position of *Lecture Assistant* explaining that my duties would be to take over his lectures when he was away, also to keep lists and attendance records of his students (he hated administration) and, if the need should arise, go to his home for a stint of baby-sitting. I decided that it would be better for me to stay at St. Andrews.

Soon after the war, Mordell left Manchester to take up a senior post at Cambridge, and the Mathematics Department at Manchester was completely transformed. It was placed under the joint leadership of **Max Newman** and **Sidney Goldstein.** They were eminent mathematicians who had used their talents with outstanding success during the war. Goldstein, an expert in aerodynamics, had made important contributions to the aircraft industry. Newman had been in charge of a section (called 'Newmanry' at the time) of the celebrated team of mathematicians at Bletchley Park who broke the German military code.

Now that the war was over Newman and Goldstein were determined to make Manchester one of the foremost centres of mathematics in the country. Their immediate task was to appoint new members to the teaching staff. The first advertisement was for the post of an applied mathematician. I was so keen to move to Manchester that I put my name forward; after all, my present position at St. Andrews was that of an applied mathematician. I was pleased that I was called for an interview and I felt that it was going well. Professor Goldstein then said: "If you get this job, you will have to do a fair amount of service teaching, especially to engineers, who have to study mathematics in some depth. Of course, also to physicists, and you may even have to teach chemists. After a short pause he added in a low voice: "Mathematically speaking, chemists are the lowest form of humanity." I promised to do my best to teach all levels of humanity and went back to St. Andrews hoping that I should soon get a favourable reply. However, a few days later a handwritten letter from Professor Newman arrived, in which he told me that the Committee had decided not to appoint me to the post of an applied mathematician. It was felt (quite correctly) that my main interest was still in the pure side, but he lessened my disappointment by adding that there would shortly be a vacancy for a lecturer in pure mathematics and that he would regard me as a very strong candidate. All I needed to do was to write to the Registrar saying that I was interested in this post. No further interview would be required. In due course I was happy to receive the confirmation that I had been appointed to a lectureship in mathematics for a probationary period of three years at an annual salary of £ 550.

Further appointments for the Department were soon authorized and, before long, all those who had been candidates at the first interview were added to the Faculty. We became close colleagues and I formed friendships with some of them which extended to our families and lasted long after we left Manchester to continue our careers elsewhere. In addition to the colleagues of whom I shall write later, the Faculty included Maurice Bartlett, Paul Cohn, Graham Higman and David Rees, who all became Fellows of the Royal Society.

Max Newman was a highly efficient and resourceful Head of Department, but his style of leadership was somewhat autocratic. At the end of the term one would find a piece of paper on one's desk saying for example: "Next term you will give a course of lectures on projective geometry", without having previously been asked whether one knows anything about the subject. At a personal level he appeared aloof and reserved; during the sixteen years that I was a member of his staff I was always "Ledermann" to him.

Yet he could also show personal consideration towards me. When we moved to Manchester in the autumn of 1946 we first stayed in furnished rooms as there was not enough time to look for a house and arrange its purchase. Evidently, Newman noticed that Rushi and I were not very comfortable, but I was surprised when, after the end of the summer term in 1947, he invited us to stay at their beautiful house at Altringham, near Manchester, while he and Mrs. Newman were on holiday in Wales. The only condition attached to this offer was that we should look after the hens they kept in their garden. In 1947 we were still being rationed and people were encouraged to supplement their food supply. I had no previous experience of keeping livestock. In particular, I did not know that hens indulge in racial discrimination: one of Newman's hens was brown, all the others being white. The brown hen was constantly being chased away from the bowl of food we used to place in the garden, so that eventually we had to provide an extra little bowl for the persecuted creature.

I believe Newman respected my experience and interest in teaching. He appointed me to be a member of a committee, chaired by him, whose task was to review the teaching of mathematics in schools. The committee sometimes met in Cambridge. The Newmans still had a house near Cambridge (Mrs. Newman was a writer and Manchester did not suit her artistic temperament). On such occasions I was his guest at their house, and he even invited me once to dinner at St. John's, his Cambridge College.

Soon after the war some of the leading British mathematicians, who included Max Newman and his friend, the charismatic Oxford topologist **Henry Whitehead**, decided it would be desirable to have an annual meeting of mathematicians in order to stimulate research and to give younger mathematicians the opportunity to be seen and heard. The meeting, henceforth to be known as the *British Mathematical Colloquium*, would be held during the academic vacation at a university that was willing and able to be the host. The programme was to be strictly confined to high-grade mathematics. There was to be no provision for entertainment or for the introduction of guests. Newman and his friends had engaged the speakers, but a great deal of administrative and domestic work had still to be done to launch the project. Remembering that I had taken part in organizing one of the Edinburgh Colloquia, Newman called me to his office one morning and said "Ledermann, I want you to make all the necessary preparations for the British Mathematical Colloquium that is to have its inaugural meeting in Manchester later this year. I want you to understand that the meeting will be devoted solely to mathematics – no wives and no dogs".

This task placed a heavy responsibility on me. After sending programmes and application forms by post, I estimated that about eighty people would attend (the membership is now several hundred). It was one of my duties to find suitable accommodation. I chose Dalton Hall, at that time a residence for male students. The house was run by the Society of Friends. Its principal at the time was **Jock Sutherland**, whose wife was the former Mary Lakeman, the lovely leader of our chamber music at St. Andrews.

I had been appointed to give tutorials at the Hall in the evenings, which gave me the opportunity to get to know personally some of our mathematics students, who were staying at Dalton Hall and they said it was a comfortable place and that the food was good. As the Hall was at some distance from the University, I hired Manchester Corporation Buses to convey the members of the Colloquium in the morning from Dalton Hall to the University and bring them back in the evening. I had also inspected and reserved suitable lecture rooms at the University and made arrangements for meals and refreshments to be served between the sessions. However, I caused panic when, only a few days before the start of the conference, I was admitted to hospital suffering from acute appendicitis. Fortunately, I was discharged just in time to receive the guests at Dalton Hall, although on doctor's order I was not allowed to carry their suitcases.

Everything appeared to be going well until Henry Whitehead strode in. Even before I could show him his room, he demanded in a firm voice: "Ledermann, where is the bar?" The extent of my failure now became apparent. I am not a tee-totaller, but the provision of alcoholic beverages did not occur to me as a prerequisite for a major mathematical conference. However, Henry Whitehead obviously had different views. I did not know he was accustomed to drinking one or more pints of beer at various times of the day. It was therefore with deep regret that I had to inform him of the strict ban on alcohol at Dalton Hall in accordance with the rules laid down by the Society of Friends.

I think Whitehead never forgave my blunder. Despite all the work I had done to organise the conference, I was immediately dropped from the organizing committee. However, the British Mathematical Colloquium continues to flourish as an important annual event. Needless to say, it is now always equipped with a bar.

By the early 1950s the mathematics staff had risen to about 30 members. There were not enough rooms to provide each of us with an individual office, so we had to share rooms. I believe the loss of privacy was amply compensated by the opportunity to enjoy closer personal relations with some of your colleagues and, in particular, to exchange ideas about research topics. Moreover, for some obscure administrative reason, we had frequently to change our room-mates, which presented us with welcome variety. During that period almost all my research papers were written either in conjunction with colleagues or as a result of discussions with them.

The Mathematics Faculty included several people who, like myself, had escaped from Nazi persecution and found refuge in Britain, and they were some of the colleagues with whom I was able to engage in research. One was **Harry Reuter**, the son of Ernst Reuter, a prominent member of the German Social Democratic party at the time of the Weimar Republic. When Hitler came to power, the Reuters left Germany to escape from political persecution. After the war, Ernst Reuter returned to Berlin and was the city's successful mayor during the Soviet blockade. In gratitude for his leadership and service one of the main squares in Berlin is now called the Ernst Reuter Platz.

Harry was sent to England in 1935 at the age of 14. He lived with the family of the Cambridge mathematician Charles Burkill. Harry was educated at the Leys School, from where he went to Trinity College Cambridge. When I first met him after his appointment at Manchester he struck me as a typical young Englishman both in appearance and in speech; for he had changed his language before the critical age, said to be about 15, after which the stigma of a foreign accent cannot be eradicated. Harry was a very fine analyst with a profound knowledge of analytical methods and a sure judgment as to how and when to apply them. My collaboration with him gave me great pleasure. In addition, my wife and I enjoyed having him and his wife Eileen as friends while we lived together in Manchester. Harry and I wrote two papers about a topic in probability theory known as Markov Processes. I was pleased to know that they were well received by experts in this field. The eminent scholar D.G. Kendall referred to them as "two path-breaking papers".

By any standards **Kurt Mahler** must be regarded as one of the most remarkable mathematicians of the 20th century mathematics. He was born in 1903 into a middle-class German-Jewish family of modest means. In early childhood he contracted tuberculosis of the knee, which rendered him lame throughout his life. As a result of his illness his schooling was irregular. But he was fond of reading. As a boy he came, by chance, across a book of geometry which fascinated him, although at the time he could hardly have understood its contents. He continued his self-study of mathematics and even started to write mathematical articles. One of these papers found its way to Carl Siegel, an eminent German mathematician. Siegel was so impressed that, together with a school teacher, he arranged for Mahler's formal education to be continued so that he could be admitted to a university. In 1927 Mahler obtained his Ph.D. degree at Frankfurt, and he also spent some time at Göttingen.

Mahler realized early that he could not survive in Nazi Germany. He went first to Holland and then to Britain, where Mordell had offered him a modest position at Manchester. He remained in Manchester when Newman and Goldstein took over the Mathematics Department. His outstanding research contributions were soon recognized: he was appointed to a Personal Chair, an honour which had never before been bestowed, and he was elected to the Royal Society.

Although Mahler could make social contact at a superficial level, he was a loner who kept himself to himself. He remained unmarried and seemed to have had few close friends. Even the number of his research students was rather small. He lived in a comfortable residence, called Donner House, which was reserved for unmarried faculty members. He arranged his life according to a strict timetable: he would go to bed every day at 9.30 p.m. even when he had guests, whom he would then pass on to a colleague "for entertainment".

Kurt Mahler

He seemed to be worried about getting enough food. On one occasion at the annual Vice-Chancellor's Reception the whole faculty were invited to a supper party in a large hall. Along the walls a set of tables bore delicious food beautifully displayed. When the doors of the hall were opened, the invited guests rushed forward to help themselves to as much as could decently be put on a plate. (Many of us had not yet overcome the greed caused by war-time deprivation.) To our surprise Mahler was already in the hall, seated behind one of the tables and lustily engorging. Evidently, the waitresses had let him in through a back door, perhaps out of pity for his disability.

Mahler had two hobbies: photography and the Chinese language. He took good photographs, especially of children, and he liked to tell us that he had mastered about 2,000 Chinese characters and could read classical Chinese stories.

Throughout his life he was occupied with mathematics. His output was enormous: at least one major research article each term. The obituary published in the Bulletin of the London Mathematical Society (Vol: 24, 381-397 (1992)) lists 221 papers written by him.

It was my good fortune that, for a time, I shared an office with Mahler. He aroused my interest in the geometry of numbers, to which he had made major contributions. I was very pleased to be a co-author with Mahler of two rather long papers on this subject, the second of which had as a third co-author **John Cassels**, whom I was very pleased to have as a colleague at Manchester.

Mahler frequently gave research lectures at the weekly seminar of the Department. His talks were well organized. Sentences that would have to be referred to subsequently were highlighted with a frame around them and the blackboard was quickly covered by a multitude of rectangles. Mahler spoke clearly, albeit with a strong German accent; what was more disconcerting was the fact that his writing had retained the features of Gothic-German script, which rendered some of the letters difficult to decipher. I remember that during one of Mahler's seminars, one of our colleagues was so irritated that he interrupted saying: "Mahler can't you write more legibly? You boast that you have mastered 2,000 Chinese characters, surely you can take the trouble to learn to write 26 English characters!"

A crisis occurred in Mahler's life when Donner House closed and he was obliged to find his own accommodation. Unfortunately, Mahler had a phobia about using the telephone and he was inexperienced in business matters. He asked me to find a house for him and to undertake all the necessary negotiations. We lived in Ashwood Avenue, a quiet street in a residential part of Didsbury in Manchester. A small house in our street was vacant. I thought this would suit Mahler, since several mathematicians apart from ourselves lived in the same street. Of course, it would be necessary for Mahler to engage a housekeeper, since he completely lacked domestic skills. I suggested that he should put an advertisement into the local paper, but I warned him that he should not emphasize the fact that an unmarried professor was seeking female assistance. However, he disregarded my warning, for a few days later he appeared at our house carrying a suitcase. He opened the suitcase and said "These are all the replies I had"; and dozens of letters from middle-aged ladies fell to the floor many accompanied by photographs.

He appointed one of the applicants to be his housekeeper, but it was a dismal failure: the woman was domineering and ordered poor Mahler about. So, after suffering for a few years, he was pleased to accept the offer of a Chair at Canberra, where he would be looked after at University House in a dignified manner. I lost touch with Mahler after his move to Australia. He obviously remained active there, because he published about seventy papers after leaving Manchester.

Despite his foreign demeanour, Mahler was strongly patriotic after he became a British subject in 1946. After the war, when the political changes were being discussed, he declared emphatically that "we should keep India and not surrender any part of our empire". All in all, Mahler could be good company. I am glad I knew him and I remember him with affection and admiration.

Bernhard Neumann joined the mathematics department at Manchester a few years after me. I remembered him and his wife well from my student days in Berlin. He was two years my senior and I always looked up to him because he was working for his doctorate while I was pursuing the more modest course for the State Examination (Teachers' Diploma). By the time he came to Manchester he had already a high reputation as an expert in group theory and he had been elected a Fellow of the Royal Society. I was very pleased when he invited me to work with him on a piece of research which led to the publication of two joint papers. This work gave me the greatest satisfaction.

Peter Hilton joined the mathematics Faculty at Manchester around 1950. As a very young man he had been a member of the code-breaking team at Bletchley. Subsequently, he was a student of Henry Whitehead at Oxford, specializing in algebraic topology. I was interested in some purely algebraic aspects of this far-reaching and fertile subject. Peter and I published several joint papers on what we called *topological ringoids*. Peter and Margaret Hilton, together with their two sons, lived in a house opposite ours in Ashwood Avenue. We soon developed a warm house-to-house friendship which, I am pleased to record, continued even after the Hiltons had left Manchester.

Bernard Neumann   Peter Hilton

With some of my other colleagues it was not mathematics but music that brought us together. Both **Arthur** and **Dorothy Stone** were members of the Mathematics Department. Arthur was an able violinist; he led the string quartet in which I played the viola. Our excellent cellist was **Nancy Lighthill,** the wife of **James** (later Sir James) **Lighthill,** who was a very good pianist. The Lighthills also lived in Ashwood Avenue, a few doors from us. Our string quartet met at their house. While we were playing there James came to our house and played piano duets with Rushi; although our drawing room was not large, we were able to find room for the beautiful Blüthner grand piano that had belonged to Rushi's parents and a Schwechten upright piano of good quality; it had been in my parents' flat in Berlin and they brought it with them when they emigrated to EnglandRushi and James attempted some quite ambitious works, such as a Beethoven piano concerto, where one pianist played the original solo part and the other played the orchestral accompaniment. In the meantime we enjoyed ourselves playing classical string quartets. At coffee time, Rushi and James joined us at the Lighthill's house.

It was a great boost to the University of Manchester when **Alan Turing** joined the Mathematics Department in 1948. He was famous for the brilliant work he had done before and after joining the team at Bletchley, and he had been awarded the O.B.E. in 1944 for his contribution to the war effort. Because of a minor speech defect he did not feel comfortable about lecturing on number theory to a large class of undergraduates, and Max Newman asked me to take over the course originally assigned to Turing. It was most stimulating to talk to him over lunch and to listen to his mathematical ideas.

One of his greatest achievements was the construction of the computer, one of the first in Britain. It occupied a large part of the top floor of the engineering building, its vast size being due to the fact an enormous number (about one thousand, if I remember rightly) of electronic valves had to be used for its construction (transistors were not yet available). He invited Rushi and me to look at this astonishing machine. In order to demonstrate its various capabilities he used a programme for the valves to play 'God save the Queen', which was very effective.

Alan Turing had run foul of the law against homosexuality, which was then still in force. In the first instance, he was put on probation provided he underwent medical treatment. Rushi helped him to find a psychiatrist who took him on as a patient. But Alan suffered a relapse and he was afraid that he might be sent to prison. On 7th June 1954, a few days before his forty-second birthday, he died from cyanide poisoning. It was generally assumed that he killed himself in order to avoid the expected humiliation. But his mother believed that his death was due to an accident, since Alan was in the habit of carrying out chemical experiments even with dangerous substances. The law that condemned homosexuality as a criminal offence was repealed some years later, but too late to save the life of one of the most brilliant mathematicians whose work had been of great benefit to mankind.

As is the custom in British universities, promotion is granted solely on the grounds of successful research. I was therefore pleased when in 1953 my position at the Faculty was raised to that of a Senior Lecturer. In due course, Max Newman asked me to take a share in the supervision of postgraduate students working for the Master's or Doctor's degree. He seemed to be of the opinion that I was a suitable person to take on the more exotic candidates. I remember a young man who came to us from Afghanistan. For the sake on anonymity I will here call him **Abdul**. He was a polite young man tall and of athletic build. It turned out later that his real talent was in the game of football. He had played for the national team of Afghanistan and was highly respected for his prowess in the game. Abdul had a degree in mathematics from a university in his own country and had applied to study under my supervision for the Master's degree in mathematics at Manchester. The initial interview with me was quite painful. "Do you know anything about the theory of groups?" Answer: "No." "Have you studied matrices?" Answer: "No." I went through several more topics in mathematics and always elicited the same negative reply. I got rather desperate and eventually picked out a well-known piece of school mathematics. "Tell me, what is the Binomial Theorem." He said meekly: "I have heard of it, Sir; but I cannot recall it." I gave him a short paper on matrices by M. Fréchet, which, surprisingly in view of the eminence of the author, contained a minor mistake. I pointed this out to Abdul and asked him to make a correction and to elaborate the problem He succeeded in doing this with a great deal of coaching. Finally, his M.Sc. thesis was accepted and he returned to Afghanistan as a proud owner of a Master's degree from a British university. According to the story which he told me subsequently, he was received by the King, who gave him a gold watch and said: "My son, any wish you express shall be granted." Abdul bowed before the King and replied: "Your Majesty, it is my wish that I shall be sent back to Manchester and register for the Ph.D. degree under the supervision of Dr Ledermann."

When shortly afterwards he turned up at Manchester, I was aghast. I said to Professor Newman: "This man is not fit to work for a Ph.D. degree. I feel that he should not be accepted as research student." But Newman replied: "Unfortunately, we cannot reject him. I had a letter from the Foreign Office supporting his application for admission. If we refuse to accept him, there will be a diplomatic incident. So, I am sorry, you have to supervise him for a PhD". Abdul was very happy to be back in Manchester, not least because he would now again be able to watch Manchester City, his favourite football club. He preferred it to Manchester United, whose followers, he said, were rather vulgar.

Of course, it was difficult to think of a research topic that was not above Abdul's capacity. I suggested a problem in the theory of group characters which required a great deal of complicated calculations. I hoped that, given his diligence and perseverance, Abdul would make some useful contributions to this problem. But progress was very slow. He came to my office almost every day and asked for some help. Then it occurred to me that **Dudley Littlewood** in Bangor was interested in a similar problem. So, I asked him whether he would accept Abdul as a research student in Bangor rather than in Manchester. But Littlewood replied saying that Abdul would be welcome to work in Bangor and receive appropriate advice; but he would have to remain registered in Manchester, so that we should have the ultimate responsibility. Although this was only of limited help I was relieved when Abdul accepted Littlewood's offer and left for Bangor. However, my joy was short-lived. After less than a month Abdul appeared in my office at Manchester. He looked rather dejected and I asked him: "How do you like Bangor?" He said: "I cannot live in Bangor." I was surprised, I thought that Bangor was a nice little town and I knew that Littlewood was friendly and helpful. "Sir, I cannot live in Bangor, because there is only Second Division football." So I had to yield to his high standards of the game and take him back as my research student, however arduous the supervision would be.

He came to my office almost every day and with my help pushed the thesis forward a line or two. One day he came when I was not at the University. At that time I shared the room with

Sandy Green. Abdul opened his heart to him and complained how hard it was to write his thesis. But after a while his face brightened up and he exclaimed: "Allah and Dr Ledermann will not let me fail." Sandy, who was aware of Abdul's passion for football, gave the appropriate answer: "You may be sure that everything will be all right in the end, because Allah and Dr. Ledermann are an unbeatable team." As always, Sandy was right. In due course, Abdul's thesis was accepted and he was awarded the PhD. degree. Of course, he was enormously pleased. He planned to get married and said: "I do not want to spend a lot of money on my wife. I shall buy a shopkeeper's daughter; a judge's daughter would be too expensive."

Abdul returned to Afghanistan and I never heard from him again. I was told that he was appointed to be vice-chancellor of a university, but belonging to the King's party, he was assassinated during the revolution which abolished the monarchy.

At this point I want to express my gratitude to **Professor Geoffrey Howson** for helping me with my reminiscences about Manchester. He was an undergraduate there in the 1950s, and a resident at Dalton Hall, where he received tutorials from me. Finally, he became a successful postgraduate student and was awarded the Ph.D. degree. His interest in these memoirs and his staunch support are invaluable to me.

The high reputation of the Manchester Mathematics Department attracted numerous visitors from this country and from abroad. I remember in particular the visit from the famous Russian mathematician **Pavel Alexandrov.** I do not remember the subject of his seminar lecture, but it was well received, although he had difficulty in speaking English, whilst he had an excellent command of German. His travel schedule made it necessary for him to spend the night at Manchester. Newman thought that rather than going to a hotel, Alexandrov would feel more comfortable if he could stay with someone who spoke German. So he asked me if Rushi and I would be willing to give hospitality to this eminent visitor. Of course, we were very pleased to do this, and Alexandrov came with us to our house in Ashwood Avenue. While Rushi prepared the supper, Alexandrov and I went for a short walk in the neighbourhood. When passing a newsagent we saw the large headlines in the evening papers announcing the successful launch of the Russian spaceship *sputnik*. I asked Alexandrov how it was possible for Russia to get ahead of America in space technology. His answer was that in the Soviet Union a young person is told to study what is useful to the country and not what he would like to study. Thus, if he shows abilities in mathematics or engineering he has to study these subjects even he prefers to do medicine. In this way, Russia acquired a large number of well-trained scientists who succeeded in building the space craft. It was evident that America agreed with this policy. For almost immediately the American government decided to expand the teaching of mathematics by providing substantial financial support, from which, incidentally, I was going to benefit a few years later.

The programme of undergraduate teaching was well organized by Newman and Goldstein. Generally speaking I enjoyed the teaching assigned to me. I had been warned during the initial interview that it would involve a certain amount of service teaching but this was not an unpleasant duty. In particular, I found that the engineering students were a responsive and serious group of men (I do not think there were any girls in the class). The only problem was that they were reluctant to buy any of the textbooks recommended in the reading list. They pointed out that, each term, the lecturer covered only a small part of the book and different books were recommended for different terms. As the books were rather expensive, it was a waste of money to invest in them because most of their content was irrelevant to the degree course. I took their point, and proposed to design a series of inexpensive paperbacks, short textbooks, each of which would cover the work of one term in one course of lectures only. These books would be more elementary than the Oliver & Boyd series of *University Texts*. In fact, they would be principally designed for students for whom mathematics was a subsidiary subject. The volumes would be of uniform price (initially five shillings) and a student would have to buy only one volume for each term of a lecture course and he would gradually build up his library. I was going to call the series a *Library of*

Mathematics. Modifying a phrase from financial policy, which was current at that time, I said; "Pay as you learn."

The manager of the University Bookshop was my friend **Ernest Hochland**. I told him about my project and he communicated it to a representative of the publishing firm Routledge & Kegan Paul. They liked my idea and gave me a contract for publishing the series. One of the first volumes to appear in print was my short volume *Complex Numbers*. At the same time the notorious novel *Lady Chatterley's Lover* by D.H. Lawrence, which had been banned for obscenity, was allowed to be published and it aroused a certain amount of curiosity. A few weeks after my book had appeared in the shop, I asked Ernest how the sale was going and he replied: "You are running neck to neck with *Lady Chatterley's Lover*". It did not remain like this, but on the whole my series was well received by the public.

In many respects, Manchester was an ideal place for my private and professional life. Of course, the most important event during this period was the birth of our son, Jonathan in 1954. Rushi's training as a Jungian psychotherapist made good progress. She had a consulting room in the house of a colleague not far from where we lived. But as the training proceeded, it became necessary to make frequent visits to London. The train journey from Manchester to London was tedious. In those days some of the trains were still pulled by steam locomotives. Jonathan, who had just started primary school, saw his mother off at the station and said: "Mummy has gone to London in a stinker." It would have been better for Rushi's sake if we were to move to London or at least somewhere near London. Moreover, there were changes in the Mathematics Department that made my work there less attractive. Most of my friends and colleagues who had joined the Department in the early years had left by 1960, in order to take up senior positions elsewhere: Peter Hilton had been appointed to the Chair at Birmingham, Harry Reuter at Durham; the Neumanns and Kurt Mahler had settled in Australia and the Stones had gone to America. In addition, Max Newman expressed the bizarre view that there was not much more to do in Algebra and that henceforth he would concentrate on Topology.

I was now planning to leave Manchester. A few applications for Chairs at London Colleges were unsuccessful; but a promising opportunity presented itself in 1962. We were on a farm holiday at Offham, a small village near Brighton, when I noticed that a major building project was being carried out in the neighbourhood. The workmen explained that they were building a university in this beautiful part of Sussex. I made some enquiries and was told that the appointment to the Chair of mathematics was to be made soon. I applied and was called for interview. But the appointment was given to Bernard Scott as the first and, at that time, the only Professor of Mathematics at the University of Sussex. He had been trained at Cambridge. Evidently, his application had strong support from the mathematical establishment.

He had seen me in the waiting room together with the other applicants before the interview and therefore knew that I was interested in the University of Sussex. Shortly afterwards, Bernard invited me to join him at Sussex as a non-professorial member of the Faculty. But he added that the Council of the University had decided that the usual hierarchy among members of the Faculty should be simplified and that there should be only Professors and Lecturers but no Readers. In my reply I stated that I was already a Senior Lecturer at Manchester and that I was unwilling to move to another university without improving my status. Accordingly I declined his offer. I was surprised when, a few days later, **John Fulton,** the Vice-Chancellor of Sussex University invited Rushi and me to visit him at his home in Brighton. As guests of the University we stayed at a nice hotel on the sea front and spent a pleasant evening with John Fulton and his wife. We discovered that I had a long-standing connection with his family. My first university appointment had been a temporary lectureship at University College Dundee in 1938. On my arrival I was introduced to the Principal of the College, whose name was Fulton. It now transpired that he was John Fulton's father. I indicated that I should be pleased to join the new university; but I expected to be offered a position that was more senior than the one I had in Manchester. John Fulton agreed and he said that he would ask the Council to reverse their decision not to have Readers. He would offer me a Readership in

Mathematics. I accepted his proposal and decided to move from Manchester to Sussex.

On my return to Manchester there was just enough time to observe the statutory time for handing in my resignation. Max Newman was very angry. He had lost quite a large number of experienced staff and he had expected me to stay. I had been in Manchester for sixteen years. There was no farewell ceremony; no glass of sherry, let alone a farewell dinner for my departure. On my last day, which was during the summer holidays, I went to my office at the University and packed all my books and papers into boxes which were sent to my home. None of my colleagues was present. **Elsie Connery**, our nice Secretary noticed how depressed I was, but she only offered this advice: "Don't indulge in self-pity; it will do you no good."

Twelve years later I saw Newman again. The twenty-fifth meeting of the British Mathematical Colloquium was held in Manchester where the first meeting took place in 1949. The organizers invited Newman and me as guests of the Colloquium because Newman had been the Chairman and I the Secretary of the first Colloquium. Then Newman was quite friendly towards me. He seemed to bear no grudge but he was deeply worried because his wife was suffering from a terminal illness at that time. I never saw him again.

IX
Sussex, 1962 – 97

To join the new University of Sussex was both an exciting and a challenging experience. The first question was: where to stay? Some of my senior colleagues said: "Do not live in Brighton. It is vulgar. Lewes is a more appropriate place." I did not want to move to Lewes because I am fond of the sea. But I then remembered meeting Mr **Arthur Block**, a nice old gentleman who was a member of the Council of the Haifa Technion and had come to Manchester to form a Technion Society in support of Israel's leading Institute of Technology. He asked me to be the Secretary of this Society, a task that I was very willing to carry out. In fact, there was a Technion Society in Manchester before there was a similar Society in London.

Mr. Block told me that he lived in Rottingdean, a charming place by the sea on the outskirts of Brighton. Looking at a local map, I noticed that there was a road that led from Rottingdean, across the Sussex Downs and ended directly in front of the Campus of the University. So it would be very easy for me to go to work by car without having to pass through any built-up areas. We found a suitable house at 1, Lenham Road East, Rottingdean and moved into it in the summer of 1962. A few alterations had to be made; in particular, the outside of the balcony had to be repainted, for which Jonathan, then aged 8, designed the colour scheme.

The University had opened the previous year, in 1961, before the campus was ready and only humanities were being taught, in rented premises at Brighton. The opening of the campus at Falmer was celebrated on a fine autumn day in 1962. We went to a magnificent party held on the lawn. Delicious refreshments were served; and a complete pig roasted on a spit. Everyone was very friendly.

The University of Sussex differed markedly from the universities with which I had been involved as a teacher or as a student. On the educational side the principal idea was that subjects should not be taught in isolation. Narrow specialization was rejected in favour of interdisciplinary studies. Thus the word 'Department' was banned and replaced by 'School of Studies'. I think the idea is perhaps more relevant to the Arts than to Science. For example, when studying Italian literature, it is helpful to be acquainted with the history, social condition, philosophy and religion of that country. To be sure, there is also important cross-fertilization in the sciences. But quite often this works in an unsymmetrical way: a competent chemist, especially if he is working on the theoretical aspect, has to have a thorough knowledge of physics; a physicist, especially if he works on the theoretical aspect, has to have a thorough knowledge of mathematics. But for many topics in physics no knowledge of chemistry is needed.

The subjects that were usually combined with mathematics were physics (in the conventional way) or economics or philosophy. Despite their educational value, some students of mathematics found it irksome to have to master subjects that were alien to their interests and talent. In my own experience when working for the State Diploma in Berlin, I had to offer physics as a second major subject in addition to chemistry and philosophy as minor subjects. It did not imbue me with a liking for these fields of learning. I sometimes put forward the argument, which was not accepted by my colleagues, that mathematicians should be exempt from learning a second subject because the very word 'mathematics' is a plural noun.

By far the most important novelty for me was having tutorials with students. Not having had the benefit of an education at Oxford or Cambridge, I had only limited experience of this highly effective and satisfying form of instruction. At Sussex we were not able to offer the one-to-one relationships available at the older universities. But our tutorial groups of no more than five students were small enough for us to get to know each student personally. I greatly enjoyed this form of teaching and I hope my students did too. It is a pity that, for financial reasons, tutorial teaching had to be abandoned at Sussex and was replaced by the less personal use of exercise classes comprising some twenty students. The mathematics lectures at Sussex were much the same as everywhere else. But students were encouraged to write essays at various stages of their course, even as part of their Final Degree. Apart from the course tutors, each student had a Personal Tutor with whom he could talk about personal matters. Rushi and I were always pleased to invite our personal students to our home.

Since many of the Founding Fathers had come from Oxford, some attempts were made to turn Sussex into a "Balliol by-the-sea" and transplant some peculiar customs from Oxford. We started by having to wear gowns when lecturing. At the very beginning some academic meetings were scheduled to take place on a Saturday morning. But Bernard objected to these on the grounds that, on a Saturday, members of Faculty should be free to play golf or else attend synagogue. The Oxford ceremony of 'leave taking' was also introduced at Sussex, initially: at the end of term each student, wearing a gown, had to appear individually at the tutor's office. He summarized the student's performance during the past term, often adding a stern admonition saying he or she should have done better. Some tutors seemed to think that they were failing in their duty if the girl students did not leave their office in tears. Mercifully, the few non-Oxbridge members of the Faculty succeeded in persuading their colleagues that these archaic practices were not appropriate in a modern university and in due course they were abandoned.

But some personal problems remained. The Government had refused to provide funds for the building of Halls of Residence for the students on the grounds that there were plenty of small guest houses near the sea front in Brighton, which were used only in the summer months when the University would not be in session. So the students should live in guest houses. The proprietors would have to accept certain conditions. Of course, there would be strict segregation of the sexes. A desk with suitable lighting would have to be provided for study. The owners of the guest houses appointed a committee whose members would negotiate with the University and in particular with the Senior Tutor **Patrick Corbett**, the worldly Professor of Philosophy. But this apparently sensible solution of the accommodation problem soon ran into difficulties.

After housing the students for one year, the representatives of the guest proprietors requested an interview with the Senior Tutor. The spokeswoman opened the meeting firmly with the words: "We do not want students in our guest houses any longer". Obviously, this was an extremely serious threat. In the absence of alternative accommodation, the University might have to close at least for some time. So Patrick tactfully enquired about the reason for their discontent. As no answer was forthcoming he suggested: "Perhaps some students are a little untidy; or they are noisy, or their radios are too loud, or (broaching a delicate subject) you object to the visitors they receive, especially late in the evening: Tell me frankly what the trouble is. I promise you that it will be treated in strict confidence." Finally, the spokeswoman responded: "It is none of these things you have mentioned," and she continued with indignation: "Do you know what the students do? They bring <u>books</u> into their bedrooms. We have been in the catering business for twenty years and more. Our guests are usually nice couples from London. They have their high-tea; then they go to the cinema and when they come back, they have a night cup and go to bed. But they never bring books into their rooms." Patrick assured them that there was nothing wicked about this habit; that some students want to continue with their work late in the evening; and the University will offer the landladies two shillings more per week to cover the cost of the additional electricity.

The ladies of the committee took their leave and all seemed to be well, but only for a short time. At the end of the next academic year they came back and declared firmly: "We do not want to have students anymore." Patrick enquired what the trouble was this time. "Do you know what they do? They have parties in their rooms. As there are not enough chairs, sometimes three big lads would sit on the mattress, which is ruined by their weight and we cannot offer the bed to our summer visitors." This was obviously a serious problem. When the matter was discussed at the Senate, the Vice-Chancellor asked the Professor of Mechanical Engineering to give his opinion as to how many 'big lads' could sit on a mattress without causing irreparable damage. However, by now the University had come to the conclusion that it was unwise to remain hostage to the landladies, and it was decided to build accommodation on the spacious and beautiful campus. Unfortunately, since the project had to be financed privately, the rent for the students was rather high.

When the University was founded, the age of majority was still 21 so that most of our students, at least during the first two years, were 'minors' and legally debarred from making certain decisions. I remember the case of a student who contracted acute appendicitis and needed an urgent operation; his parents were in South Africa and could not easily be contacted. So, the Senior Tutor had to give consent to the operation in place of the parents. On one occasion Rushi and I had to go to the Registry Office to act as witnesses for the wedding ceremony for two of our students. Another aspect of the paternalistic regime was the rule that students were not allowed to be absent overnight from their lodgings, unless they had obtained prior permission (an exeat) from the Senior Tutor. Fortunately, all these troublesome restrictions were abandoned once all students had become adults in law.

When mathematics was first taught at Sussex in 1962, the Mathematics Faculty consisted of five members: **Bernard Scott** as the Professor, myself as a Reader and three Lecturers: **Ruth Rogers, Kathleen Trustrum** and **Brian Trustrum.** It was a little odd that all three Lecturers were specialists in Hydrodynamics, a subject initially not in our syllabus. But we were all willing to adapt to the task of building up a sensible course of mathematics which would fit into the idea of this new and forward looking university. I think that, on the whole, we succeeded. A great deal of credit should be given to Bernard for his guidance and determination. His style of leading the mathematics 'subject group' was, on the face of it, democratic: there was a Faculty meeting every Monday morning during which coffee and biscuits were served. We discussed Faculty business, for example lecture schedules, in a relaxed and friendly manner, but when it came to make crucial decisions, Bernard expected his opinion to prevail.

The Mathematical Faculty grew very rapidly. Of course, most of my colleagues were much younger than I was. Indeed, apart from the Vice-Chancellor, I was the oldest member of the University. It is therefore not surprising that I was asked to sit on a large number of committees that dealt with administrative matters and with the welfare of the students. I recall one particular week in which I spent 25 hours in committee meetings. I thought this was unfair, since a

Reader should use his time principally for teaching and research. It would have been different if I had been a Professor, who is expected to devote a reasonable amount of time to administration. I made this point to **Roger Blin-Stoyle**, the Professor of Physics and Dean of the School of our School. He was sympathetic to my argument, and on 1st April 1965 I was appointed to Professor of Mathematics. I was told later that the Astronomer Royal objected to my appointment because 'I was too old'. But Bernard supported me strongly and the objection was overruled.

DAVID BERNARD SCOTT (1915–1993)

Soon more professors were appointed, who specialized in Analysis, Applied Mathematics and Statistics Our mathematics group was well respected. As a result of Bernard's reputation, we received distinguished visitors from abroad, who offered interesting courses of lectures. After a few years it was decided that the Chairmanship should be held in rotation. The Chairman should be elected by his colleagues, and did not need to have a professorial rank, and should hold the position for three years. When my turn came in 1972-5, there were forty-two mathematicians at Sussex, including six professors. We all got on well with one another. Our excellent secretaries contributed a great deal to the smooth running of the School, both for the members of Faculty and for the students. My sincere thanks are due especially to **Christine Glasson** and to **Sue Bullock** for their unfailing help.

My teaching commitments occupied more of my time than at Manchester and St. Andrews. In addition to the formal lectures, I saw several of the small tutorial groups each week and I talked to my personal students whenever the occasion arose. The students who wrote essays required preliminary instruction followed by supervision and assessment. Throughout the University great importance was given to a high standard in teaching. Being one of the senior members of the Faculty I was put in charge of a committee to look into ways of improving the teaching. With their permission I attended lectures given by my colleagues and made some suggestions. But in my report I concluded sadly that "good lecturers are born and not bred".

The Mathematics Faculty also provided help outside the University. Bernard Scott was instrumental in founding the Sussex Branch of the Mathematical Association, which catered for school teachers in the area. It became a flourishing society. We often attended its meeting and sometimes gave a talk. As in other parts of the country, there was a dearth of capable mathematics teachers in our area. So Bernard arranged refresher courses for teachers. These were well attended by teachers from schools all over Sussex and I was one of their lecturers on several occasions. As far as the younger age groups were concerned, we offered master classes for pupils aged about fourteen years. These were held at the University on Saturday mornings. I was very pleased to contribute a course on *amusing arithmetic*. After a short introduction, I set some problems. The students were then divided into small groups and supervised by a teacher who helped them to solve the problems. I think the scheme was quite successful.

Another teaching commitment was associated with the Arts/Science Scheme. It was considered desirable that all arts students should attend some lectures on science or mathematics, and that conversely all science students should have some acquaintance with arts subjects. I attempted to give some lectures on mathematics that I thought would be of interest to arts students. I think my efforts were only moderately successful. In any event, the scheme was soon abandoned, because the arts tutors were unwilling to expose their students to any contact with science or, even worse, to mathematics.

A more rewarding and worthwhile form of teaching was part of the European Course: the more able students at Sussex were encouraged to follow a four-year course for the B.Sc. degree. This involved spending their third year at a university in a European country where they continued studying their major subject; at the end of that year they were required to write a dissertation in the foreign language which counted towards their degree assessment at Sussex. After their return from abroad, the students continued their course at Sussex leading to a B.Sc. degree. The local authorities had agreed to provide financial support for this extra year. Most of the students who had volunteered for the European course chose to go to France; but a small number wanted to go to Germany and an even smaller number to Italy. It was a condition that they had an A-level qualification in the language of the country of their choice. But we realized that, although they might have a good knowledge of the written and spoken foreign language, they would not be familiar with technical mathematical terms in French, German or Italian. So it was decided that in the year prior to their departure the students on the European course should have one tutorial a week in the foreign language. It was fortunate that the Faculty could provide this service; one of my colleagues had spent some time in the French speaking part of Canada and another colleague had done some research in Rome. I was willing to give tutorials in German, which I quite enjoyed although it was more than forty years since I had been a student in Germany.

Because my first degree, or its equivalent, was taken at a German university in the 1930s, I was never presented with an unseen paper from which I had to answer a specified number of questions in two or three hours. It is therefore somewhat ironical that, after I had reached a certain seniority at a British university, I was asked to act as external examiner by a rather large number of universities in the British Isles. They included Edinburgh, Glasgow, Keele, Canterbury, Southampton, Birmingham, Wales, the Open University and the National University of Ireland. Each appointment was for three or four years; in some cases two visits were required in a year. So the number of journeys I made as an external examiner must have added up to about forty. The duties of an external examiner involve scrutinizing and commenting on the draft of the questions before the examination and consulting with the resident colleagues what grades were to be awarded to the candidates after the examination. The work was not particularly arduous. After all, routine questions did not differ greatly from one year to the next and from one university to another.

Without exception, my visits as external examiner were pleasant experiences. Quite often I was offered hospitality by one of the resident colleagues, even with chamber music when I was staying with **Hans Liebeck** in Keele. The examiners' meetings at which the assessments of the candidates were decided were always conducted in a friendly manner; I never encountered any controversies or disputes. My appointment to the University of Wales involved visits to Cardiff and Swansea. Each place had its own examination papers, which I had to approve. My examiner's duties for Ireland were even more numerous, for the National University of Ireland consisted of colleges in Cork, Dublin and Galway each setting different examination questions that I had to scrutinize. Moreover, only one examiner in mathematics was appointed. His services were required for assessment of a course of Elementary Mathematics, an Honours Course in Mathematics, a Doctorate in Mathematics and some mathematical work at a Theological College. Examinations were held in June and in September, and the external examiner was expected to be present on both occasions. So during my tenure of this office I was kept rather busy.

Early in the year numerous registered parcels arrived with the draft of the questions. My secretary felt quite sorry for me. "Yet another parcel has arrived from Ireland", she said. But I consoled her: "Don't worry, Ann. In the last century Gladstone was troubled by the Irish Question, but I am not bothered by a hundred Irish

Questions." I started my tour of duties at Cork. After that I spent some very pleasant days in Dublin and finally travelled by taxi to Galway. Everywhere I was received with warm hospitality. After my last visit as External Examiner, Rushi joined me, and we had a delightful holiday in the beautiful Irish countryside.

My association with the Open University lasted eight years, during which I acted as External Examiner for the course known a 'M335'. At the end of this period I was presented with an attractive tankard on which the following words were engraved: *Walter: The Open University, For 8 happy years of M335*. I also examined for other courses, and acted as an advisor and assessor for the construction of new courses. To my surprise and delight the Open University conferred on me the Degree of Honorary Doctor in 1993. The Degree Ceremony was held in Edinburgh, where 53 years earlier I had received the Doctor of Science degree, but on that occasion, because of the war, no ceremony was held and the Certificate was handed to me in a corner of the University Library.

It was a pleasure to be invited by a foreign university to take part in a conference or to give a lecture, sometimes even a course of lectures. My most extensive visits were to the United States of America. When I was still in Manchester, **Saunders MacLane** invited me to Chicago for a few weeks to talk about my recent work with Peter Hilton. It was my first experience of America. On the whole, my visit to Chicago was very pleasant. I enjoyed the beautiful shores of Lake Michigan and the superb Art Collection (at the Art Institute). All people I met were friendly and hospitable. But there were also some less agreeable moments.

I first went to New York, to visit my Uncle Ernst (my mother's younger brother). I had my violin with me because I hoped to play some music in Chicago. When I got off the aeroplane I was seized by two excited customs officials, who got hold of my violin case shouting: "What is in there?" I was surprised and answered innocently: "A violin." I was ignorant of the fact that gangsters often carry their gun in a violin case. I arrived in Chicago on a Sunday. The weather was hot and I decided to go for a swim in one of the public beaches along the shores of the lake. When I came out of the changing room, I noticed that an armed policeman was on guard and that I was the only white person on the beach. On the next day I told MacLane where I had been and he said: "You should not go there. It is a beach for blacks."

Several more visits to the United States were to follow. After the Russian triumph with their Sputnik, the American government decided to increase the number of people who were good mathematicians and who could make the subject more popular. The National Science Foundation (NSF), which is funded by the government, instructed several universities in the States to hold refresher courses in the summer vacation. These courses were, in the first instance, intended for school teachers of mathematics, who were given the opportunity to improve their knowledge of mathematics. One of the places selected for such a refresher course was the **University of Notre Dame** in Indiana. I do not know why I was recommended to be one of the teachers for their summer course, but I was pleased to accept the invitation in 1962, and the following two years.

Unfortunately, Rushi and Jonathan could not come with me. The University of Notre Dame is situated in a large beautiful campus, not far from South Bend, a small provincial town. It can be reached fairly easily from Chicago. The university is a Roman Catholic institution. Most faculty members were Roman Catholics and many were priests (Fathers), except the Chairman of Mathematics, **Arnold Ross**, who was of Russian-Jewish origin. He was devoted to teaching and to awakening people's interest in mathematics. It was his ingenious idea to invite to the refresher course a selected group of gifted high school boys aged about 15. I gave my lecture early in the morning because it used to get very hot later in the day. After my lecture I went to the excellent indoor swimming pool, reserved for men in the morning and for women in the afternoon. There were rather exaggerated rules for hygiene: bathers were not allowed to use their own swimming trunks and towels. They had to take a shower, watched by an attendant, who then gave them white swimming trunks and a bath towel. When I collected my linen parcel from him, he said deferentially: "Here you are, Father."

I offered to give a simple course on group theory. Many members of my class wanted to buy a copy of my textbook *Introduction to the Theory of Groups*, published by Oliver & Boyd in Edinburgh. The manager of the University Book Shop, thought it would be simplest to order a consignment of fifty copies direct from the publishers in Edinburgh. This was promptly done, and a rather large package arrived at the Airport in Chicago. But now an unforeseen difficulty arose. It was the height of the Cold War and the anti-communist witch hunt in America. The custom official inspected the consignment of my book. Evidently, he did not understand the contents. The title was suspicious: *Theory of Groups -* what groups? He must have thought that what this foreign author had in mind are probably 'Groups of Communists or Anarchists'. So, the whole consignment was confiscated; it was released only after intervention by the President of the University, and the books reached my students, albeit belatedly.

The University of Notre Dame played host to eminent mathematicians from many countries and they were always received with warm hospitality I met many interesting people there. On one occasion, the guest was a famous Polish mathematician who spoke little English. As usual, a dinner was given in his honour and before the meal started, the Chairman went to the place where the guest was sitting and said: "Professor, would you like to have Rosé tonight?" "With a gleam in his eye the visitor chuckled: "Why not – if she is pretty!" The University was also famous for its excellence at football. I felt very much honoured when after one of my visits I was presented with a sweater bearing the insignia of the celebrated team. Needless to say, I never had the chance to wear this shirt.

At the end of my second year at Notre Dame I was offered a permanent position as Professor of Mathematics. (I was still a Reader at Sussex.) I was touched by the trust my colleagues at Notre Dame had in me but I declined the tempting invitation because I felt that my family and I would not be happy settling in a provincial town in America. Although everyone at Notre Dame was very kind to me it was nevertheless a strange surrounding for me. In any case, I am too much a European. At about the same time I was offered a Chair in Australia which I declined for the same reason.

In 1963 Arnold Ross left Notre Dame and accepted the Chair of `Mathematics at Columbus, Ohio. He was going to continue the summer programme there and invited me to join him the following year, which I was very pleased to do. As always, I received a generous fee for my work and on this occasion it was possible for Rushi and Jonathan to join me in America after I had finished my lectures. I met them in New York, and we travelled across the States to California with a visit to Disney Land as a special treat for Jonathan. I regret that this was my last teaching engagement in America. One of the people I met at Chicago was the Danish mathematician **Svend Bungaard** from the University of Århus, a pleasant town on the East coast of Jutland overlooking the Baltic. He invited me to lecture in Denmark and Rushi and Jonathan accompanied me on this occasion. After I had completed my course of lectures we had an enjoyable trip to Copenhagen before returning to Sussex.

Several foreign journeys were due to invitations from countries following requests by former students. I was a guest speaker at a meeting of the Iranian Mathematical Society and it was agreed that instead of paying a fee, the Society would arrange for me to have a tour of the country, which enabled me to see some of the beautiful historical places of ancient Persia. On another occasion, a student from Bangladesh, who had enjoyed his stay at Sussex, made arrangements for my colleague **Gavin Wraith** and me to be invited to address a meeting of the Bangladesh Mathematical Society, which was held in Dacca, the capital of the country. We had a friendly reception, but the poverty and drabness of the place was rather depressing.

An interesting but only moderately enjoyable experience was my participation at the International Congress of Mathematicians in Moscow in 1966. The lecture rooms were overcrowded and uncomfortable and I did not attend many lectures. But I saw a very good performance of a ballet. Since the University of Sussex had nominated me as the official delegate, I was privileged to have a personal guide; he was a young Russian student who spoke excellent English. However, there were limitations regarding what he was allowed to show me. When visiting the Art Gallery, which I believe, houses a large collection of beautiful classical paintings, I was permitted to see only the contemporary 'socialist' pictures. One day I saw a long queue stretching along a street in the centre of the town. I asked my guide why these people are queuing and he said: "They want to see the body of Lenin which is displayed in the mausoleum." I was not particularly keen to see this exhibit, but my guide thought that it would be appropriate to take me to the mausoleum. He took me to the head of the queue and exchanged a few words with the armed soldiers guarding it. We were immediately allowed to go to the head of the queue. When we entered the mausoleum my guide said: "You must not speak now, just think you are in a church." We entered the room where the dead body of Lenin lay in a glass coffin. He was dressed in a suit which had been the fashion in the 1920s. At the end of the Congress I had a few rubles left and I wanted to buy a bottle of genuine Russian Vodka to take home with me, but the shop in the hotel refused to accept the national currency. I was told that anything taken out of the country had to be paid for in 'dollars'.

In 1974 I made a memorable visit to Mexico. A few years earlier **Araceli Reyes de Gonzales** had come to Sussex with her husband **Cesar**, a physicist, who was then engaged in a research project in this country. She had a first degree in Mathematics from a university in her country and I suggested to her that she might continue her studies of mathematics at Sussex University and preferably work for a doctorate. I chose a topic that I thought would suit her and I supervised her research. In due course she obtained the D.Phil. Degree from Sussex. She and Cesar had become friends of our family. After returning to Mexico, she was appointed to a senior position, and on her initiative I was invited to give a course of lectures at the University of Mexico (in English, since I do not speak Spanish). After my course, for which I received a generous fee, Rushi joined me and we had a most interesting trip, taking us to many places in this fascinating country. A little later Jonathan and Sarah, his girlfriend and also a medical student, joined us and they too toured the country.

The most rewarding trip abroad was my visit to Israel in 1972. I had just been elected Chairman of the Mathematics Faculty at

Sussex and I had asked my colleagues to give me sabbatical leave for one term before I had to begin the administrative duties which my new position would entail. I stayed with my sister Ruth, in Kiryat Tivon, a pleasant town on a hill near Haifa. Our mother lived in an old-age home nearby. I had been invited to give some lectures at the Israel Institute of Technology (the Technion) in Haifa. It was quite easy to travel from Tivon to Haifa, as there was a regular bus service. The subject of my course was *Group Representations*: based on a course given by Issai Schur in Berlin in 1931. Since I do not speak Hebrew, I lectured in English. The secretary of the Technion was very helpful. She rapidly produced a typewritten version of my lecture notes, which was bound as a book and was offered to the students at a small fee. Somehow a copy of this book found its way to the editors of the Cambridge University Press. They wrote to me and asked whether I would agree to them publishing my Haifa Notes as a book. Of course, I was pleased to accept the offer but I pointed out that the Haifa Technion had the copyright, and a publication could only go ahead with permission from the Technion. This was graciously granted and I stipulated that any royalties from the sale of my book should be shared between the Technion and myself. I do not know whether, during the four hundred years of its existence, the Cambridge University Press had ever entered into such arrangement. The book was published in 1977, followed by a second enlarged edition ten years later.

The *Library of Mathematics* ('penny shockers') which I started in Manchester continued to grow after I had moved to Sussex. New volumes were written by some of my colleagues at Sussex but also by mathematicians, who I met during my visits as external examiner or who were recommended to me. I edited all these books, and I was pleased that the series eventually comprised more than twenty titles. It is a great pity that when Routledge & Kegan Paul was taken over by a large American firm, the whole series was taken out of print, because there was not enough profit in 'cheap & nasty' little books, however much they were appreciated by the students. I had invested a great deal of thought and time into producing these textbooks and I was disappointed that my efforts were swept aside by commercial greed.

However, my wish to communicate mathematics to a wider audience found another outlet. On one of his routine visits to the University of Sussex a representative of the publishers John Wiley & Sons asked me if I would like to write a textbook to be published by Wiley. I told him that, in my opinion, Wiley's books were too expensive for most students. Instead, I suggested that I might act as editor of a comprehensive reference work for people who are not mathematicians but who use mathematics in their profession including physicists, engineers, statisticians, psychologists, economists and many others. My idea was to provide a simple exposition of 'useful' or 'applicable' (not 'applied') mathematics. The idea appealed to the director of Wiley and I received a contract to go ahead with the project which I called a *Handbook of Applicable Mathematics*.

The intention was to present the mathematical material in *Core Volumes*, one for each branch of mathematics, such as Algebra, Analysis, Geometry and Probability. The Core Volumes were to be supplemented by *Guide Books*, each referring to a profession, in which mathematics is used and where references would be given to the appropriate section of the core volumes, such as *Mathematical Methods in Economics*. It was a formidable task. But I was extremely fortunate to be supported by a very able and friendly Editorial Board. It included **Robert Churchhouse**, whom I knew from his student days at Manchester. He took charge of the volume on *Numerical Methods*. **Emlyn Lloyd,** of the University of Lancaster, edited the Core Volumes on *Probability* and *Statistics*. The other Core Volumes were edited jointly by **Steven Vajda** from Sussex University and myself. Peter Hilton represented the *Handbook* in the United States, and I was pleased that he was able to attend some of the meetings of the Editorial Board during his visits to England. My work was greatly helped by **Carol Alexander** (then **Carol van der Ploeg**), as the devoted and highly efficient Assistant Editor.

The meetings of the Board were organized and chaired by **Jamie Cameron** who was appointed by John Wiley to be our editor. The meetings, at Wiley's expense, took place at a West End Club, where Jamie was a member. The Club had rather strict rules regarding the admission of visitors. On one occasion, when Peter Hilton turned up in an open neck shirt, he was refused entry, and we had to go to a gentlemen's outfitter where Jamie bought a proper shirt and tie for Peter (again at Wiley's expense). It happened to be quite an appropriate occasion because it was Peter's birthday. The meetings were always conducted in a very amicable manner, and I felt that I was among friends. The first Core Volume appeared in 1980, and the series was concluded with the Index Volume, published in 1991. As there were several years of planning before publication began the Editorial Board met regularly for about fifteen years. We produced six *Core Volumes* and a *Supplement*, together amounting to about 5000 pages. The articles in the *Core Volumes* were written by 60 authors, not all of them from the United Kingdom.

Numerous review articles about the *Handbook of Applicable Mathematics* ('Ham' for short) appeared in journals throughout the world. The assessment was usually quite favourable. Furthermore, I believe Wiley was satisfied with the commercial aspect of the project. Indeed, when I spoke to the Manager of Wiley he commented: "The Handbook of Applicable Mathematics is our flagship." I visited Wiley's office at Chichester several times and I was always made very welcome. The racecourse Glorious Goodwood is situated near Chichester and Wiley owns a beautiful room overlooking the racecourse. On one occasion Rushi and I were invited to join them there to watch one of the races (a unique experience for us). We were welcomed by the Duke of Richmond who owns the course. Rushi placed a bet on a horse and won one pound.

Wiley's main office is in New York. During my work on our joint project I was sent there (at their expense) to discuss matters of common interest with the management in America, and during my visit I stayed at the luxurious Wiley Apartment in Manhattan. On another occasion Wiley sent me to represent the company at a conference on publication which was held at an attractive former castle in East Germany. At the conference dinner I sat next to a mathematician and enquired about my former colleague Klaus Fuchs who now lived in East Germany. My host promptly gave me a kick under the table and whispered: "don't talk to that man about him, he works as a spy".

In addition to my work as editor of 'Ham', I was engaged by Wiley as one of its advisors on mathematics. For a modest annual salary, I was asked to give my opinion on proposals for the publication or translation of mathematical texts. One of these was by the French mathematician **Françoise Chatelin** on *'eigenvalues'*. I thought her book would be of considerable interest to English readers and since the topic was in my field of interest, I offered to do the translation myself. It was the only time that I have done this kind of work. Evidently, it was quite well received because my English version had two editions. I was sad when my contact with Wiley came to an end after more than twenty years. It had been a most valuable experience. I was grateful for my long friendship with the members of the editorial board and the contributors of the mathematical articles, and I enjoyed the contacts with the appreciative and supportive staff at the Chichester Office.

Considering the effort which the mathematics Faculty members at Sussex expended when teaching and caring for our students, both on an academic and on a personal level, it is perhaps not surprising that mathematical research took second place. This was partly due to a lack of leadership. When I was appointed to the Chair, I believe that some of my younger colleagues expected me to arrange weekly Research Seminar meetings, during which recent papers or books would be discussed and further research would be stimulated. I cannot explain why I did not do this, and I regard this failure as a blot in my career. The mathematics subject group produced less original work than members teaching other subjects, notably the chemists who soon counted several Fellows of the Royal Society in their group; no mathematician was ever elected to the Royal Society while at Sussex.

Nevertheless our strength in analysis, which was led by the professors **David Edmunds** and **Peter Bushell** attracted some excellent researchers, particularly from Russia during the 1990's. Regrettably, several newly appointed faculty members eventually left Sussex, because they wanted to be at a university where more encouragement is given to research. These include Professor

Dimitri Vassiliev, who kindly arranged an honorary professorship for me at University College London, where he now holds the Chair of Mathematics.

It was a tragedy for British mathematics and a disgrace to the University of Sussex that the School of Mathematical Sciences was closed down in 2003. A group of sixteen members, led by Professor **Charles Goldie**, was moved to the School of Engineering and continued to teach what mathematics was still deemed necessary. I keep in touch with this group to this day, as Charles visits me in London regularly. The scale of destruction of Mathematics at Sussex can be measured by comparing the situation at the University of St. Andrews, where the Mathematics Faculty has seventy-six members, including nineteen professors.

The statutory age of retirement for university posts is 65 years, which I reached in 1976. My successor, was duly appointed, but he was in the middle of a Royal Society research contract and was debarred from undergraduate teaching for the next two years. So Lord **Asa Briggs,** who was Vice Chancellor at that time, asked me to come to his office and said: "Walter, you have hardly changed, since I first met you about fifteen years ago. I suggest you carry on in your position for another two years until your successor can take up his duties." Of course, I was very pleased to accept this offer. However, as I discovered later, some of my colleagues, mainly physicists, resented the Vic-Chancellor's decision, which, they said was high-hander and should have first been considered by the Faculty. I am pleased to say, however, that I was not aware of any hostility among my mathematical colleagues.

I trust that I have done my fair share in supervising research students, all of whom were successful in obtaining the D.Phil. degree. This was the kind of work that gave me great satisfaction. I also had the pleasure of being the joint author of several research papers with my students. I continue to work with my last student, Carol Alexander, and so far we have published two papers: one on a topic in pure mathematics which derived from her dissertation and a second one after she had taken a Masters degree in Mathematical Economics and Econometrics at the London School of Economics and returned to Sussex as a member of the Faculty, when we cooperated on a game-theoretic investigation into an economic problem.

Considerable demands on my time and energy were made by the publication of textbooks, and later by editing the Handbook (details of my books are available in the 'open library' on the internet, although I do not know who put them there). Nevertheless, I have always tried to remain active in research. Steven Vajda and I published a paper on a statistical question of interest to him. When the paper appeared in print, Steven was ninety years old and I had passed my eightieth birthday. But this may not be my last research paper to be published. In 2007, as I was reading the manuscript of Carol Alexander's four-volume textbook on *Market Risk Analysis*, I became interested in correlation matrices because they play an important role in the subject. I found that one of their properties seems to have been overlooked, and this led to the introduction of an orthogonal matrix that can be used to generate samples which have, exactly, a given correlation matrix. At the same time, my grandson Daniel was starting his doctorate research under Carol's supervision. I am very glad that my result has provided a basis for Daniel's thesis, which introduces a new simulation technique based on random orthogonal matrices (ROMs). Unlike Monte Carlo, ROM simulation makes no parametric assumptions and targets, without sampling error, the multivariate sample moments.

In 1978 my official retirement became inevitable. I was touched by the immense generosity and goodwill when my retirement was celebrated. I knew that the main driving force behind all this was Bernard Scott, and I am deeply grateful to him for the friendship shown to me, especially as in our professional life we did not always fight on the same side of the barricades.

On 17th June 1978, a Supper Party was held in my honour at the University Refectory, 7.00-11.00 p.m. Guests were received by Sir **Denys Wilkinson**, who was the Vice Chancellor at that time. It was a truly magnificent occasion. Bernard had written to all my former students and to many of my friends who were not at Sussex. A booklet was published: *Walter Ledermann. University of Sussex 1962-1978* listing 309 names of those who had replied to the invitation, whether or not they were able to come to the party. From the collection (not more than 50p each) I was given a beautiful Swiss watch, which I still wear. One student wrote to say that since I often make mistakes when carrying out numerical work on the black board, it would be appropriate that I should be given a pocket calculator. This was duly done and I still have it! During the party, chamber music was performed by a group of colleagues and former students, and flowers were presented to Rushi. **Arthur Craven**, who was Chairman of Mathematics at that time, made a very friendly speech. He said: "Although this is a retirement party for Walter, I do not believe that he will actually retire from being active as a mathematician." He was right: I remained in Sussex for another 18 years giving occasional courses and keeping in touch with colleagues and students.

X
Final Retirement: London 1997

After Rushi had celebrated her eightieth birthday, it became clear that the time had come for her to retire from her work as a psychotherapist. We both felt that it would be prudent to move to London, so that we could be near our family. Jonathan, who is always so willing to help us, would obviously find it easier to visit us when we lived in the same neighbourhood instead of having to make the two hour journey to Sussex.

We went to several estate agents in Highgate, north London and wanted to buy a small, three-roomed flat in the area. However, there was one difficulty. At that time (in 1996) Rushi still very much enjoyed playing the piano; in fact what she liked best was to play pieces for two pianos. In our house at Hove we had a beautiful Blüthner grand piano and a good, though rather old, upright Bechstein. Rushi had several friends who were pleased to play the lovely Sonata for two pianos by Mozart with her, and other music for two pianos. So, we told the estate agents that one of the rooms in our flat should be big enough to have two pianos in it. This condition was greeted with skepticism. We had to make several visits to their offices and Rushi became known as "the lady with the two pianos". Eventually, we found what we wanted: a flat on the first floor of the rather prestigious block of flats in Highgate, known as Highpoint; it was then a Grade II listed building and has now been classified as Grade I. The lounge or music room, as we call it, was indeed big enough for the two pianos.

Otherwise the flat is not particularly beautiful. The front room faces the street and the back room looks towards the wall of another part of the building. Accommodation in London is of course more expensive than in Sussex. The sale of our eight-room house in Hove raised less money than the price for the three-roomed flat in Highgate. The purchase of the flat was effected through a "developer" who tried to maximize his profit. It was part of the sale that the kitchen would be refitted and that a washing machine and a dishwasher would be installed. In the front room double-glazed

130

windows were to be installed, in order to reduce the noise from the street. Unfortunately, we discovered too late that much of the material used by the shifty businessman was of inferior quality and had to be replaced soon afterwards at our expense.

Finally, after having sold our house in Hove, we arrived on the appointed day to take possession of our flat at Highpoint. But we were told that regrettably there had been some delay with the decorators and the paintwork was still wet. So we had nowhere to live. To make the best of this misfortune, we went to Perugia for two weeks. After returning from this delightful holiday we finally moved into our new home with 102 packing cases. There was still a great deal to be done: wardrobes and bookcases had to be built in; curtains and carpets had to be bought. But in the end we were satisfied with our choice and were ready to settle in.

Highpoint has several pleasant features. There is a large and well-kept garden at the rear with an outdoor swimming pool that is heated to a very acceptable temperature from May until October. Even if one does not go into the water (I have done so only once), it is enjoyable to sit down by the side of the pool and enjoy the (rare) sunshine. The handsome entrance hall and the stair carpets are in good condition and are always clean. A helpful porter is on duty all day. Unlimited hot water is available at any time. This is included in the 'service charge', as is the heating of the flat, which is done through under floor heating; there are no radiators in the rooms, so that the amount of heating is not under our control. All in all, we found that Highpoint provided comfortable living.

Our main reason for moving to London was that to see more of our family. This hope has been fully realized; Jonathan and Sarah have been most kind and generous towards us and we are delighted to see our grandchildren grow up and we share in their many successes. Jonathan is always ready to give practical help, especially when I struggle with the computer. Being in London has also made it easier for us to see other relatives and friends. My brother Erich lived in Hampstead, and after his wife's death we visited him once a week. Most sadly, Erich died in 2005 and I miss him very much. Rushi's cousins **Peter Sinclair** (from her mother's side) and **Pali Schlesinger** (on her father's side) both lived in Pinner. We made

131

the journey a few times and kept in touch until Pali moved to the North of England, where he died. We also visited Rushi's friends, **Anne Barua** and **Paula Bar** who live near Swiss Cottage.

Since moving to London, we have been able to enjoy its superb artistic life. We became Friends of the National Gallery and of the Tate Gallery and saw many beautiful exhibitions there. The Sunday morning concerts at the Wigmore Hall were always enjoyable. We often went there with friends and had lunch with them afterwards. We were able to travel to Switzerland for our summer holiday, staying at our favourite hotel in Flims. I also kept in touch with Sussex University and Rushi and I attended the Christmas party at the School of Mathematics. We also took part in the celebration on Graduation Day.

Alas, all these activities ceased about 2002 when Rushi's infirmity and our old age took their toll. For a few years we could still use a mini cab service to visit relatives and friends, but journeys to places outside London are no longer possible. We have indeed been very fortunate that the Agency *Companions of London* sent us **Carmen Durgacharan** as a carer. Her devotion, expertise and friendship are invaluable to us. She now comes twice every day for a few hours in the morning and in the evening, even on Saturdays and Sundays. Without her help our lives would be much harder.

After re-reading these pages I believe that I have good reason to be satisfied with my life and career. There were many situations and events for which I am truly grateful. My childhood was spent in a secure and supportive home, where our family lived with very little tension. It was most fortunate that I had no difficulty with schoolwork and, as a consequence, was awarded the Leaving Certificate six months before the usual time. It became apparent later that this was crucial for my future; for it enabled me to go to university early and gain my State Diploma. Had it been later, it would have been impossible to do this under the Nazis. The most miraculous stroke of luck that probably saved my life, was Erich's discovery that the University of St. Andrews was offering a scholarship to one Jewish refugee from Germany. I could hardly believe it when I received a letter from the World Student Service in Switzerland informing me that I had been chosen for this award. On

3rd January 1934 I left my native city and travelled to St. Andrews. Henceforth Britain became my home, a change for which I am profoundly grateful. My professional activities have given me much satisfaction. I know that I am not one of the great mathematicians of our epoch, but I trust that I have been of help to some of my students and that my published work has met with some appreciation. I very much enjoyed the time with my students and the stimulating company of colleagues with whom I conducted research.

However, by far the greatest blessing was the happiness with my family. My marriage to Rushi, now in its sixty-second year is based on love and mutual respect. It was crowned by the birth of Jonathan. The care and support which he and Sarah give us are of inestimable help in our old age. Our delightful grandchildren are a constant source of pleasure. If I could have my life again, I should not wish it to be much different.